A Basic Grammar of Modern Spoken Tibetan

a practical handbook

by

TASHI

LIBRARY OF TIBETAN WORKS AND ARCHIVES

First Printed 1990
Reprinted 1994

ISBN 81-85102-74-0
Typeset by computer at LTWA

Published by the Library of Tibetan Works and Archives, Dharamsala and printed at Indraprastha Press (CBT), 4 Bahadur Shah Zafar Marg, New Delhi-110 002

FOREWORD

One of the many responsibilities assigned to LTWA at its inception nearly twenty years ago was to provide facilities for the study of the Tibetan language. Accordingly classes have been offered which have been attended by several hundred people from countries all over the world. To begin with there were few text books designed for foreigners to learn Tibetan, so it has also been LTWA policy to develop such materials and consequently a number of books and tapes have been published.

Tashi Daknewa is one of LTWA's resident Tibetan language teachers and with twelve years classroom experience, as well as a one year sabbatical teaching and studying in the USA, he has developed a keen awareness of students' needs. Through diligently noting the many and various questions he has been asked over the years, as well as the answers he gave, he has been able to compile this book, which illustrates Tibetan grammar from a quite fresh perspective. What he has tried to do is to address the problems that occur in students' minds when initially presented with Tibetan grammar in the traditional way.

Tashi is to be congratulated for his initiative and dedication and it is my fervent hope that by easing the linguistic difficulties somewhat this book will contribute to international understanding and friendship for Tibet and her people.

Gyatsho Tshering
Director
LTWA

PREFACE

A Basic Grammar of Modern Spoken Tibetan is written for those non-Tibetan who have a keen interest in learning the proper rules of spoken Tibetan grammar. This book is based on my twelve years of experience in teaching Tibetan language at the Library of Tibetan Works and Archives, Dharamsala and one year teaching and studying in the U.S.A. During these years I have collected several notes which express the common grammatical problems of Tibetan language students. In this book I have tried to present the grammar rules as clearly as possible with a number of simple examples, so that it may be used by anyone who has no previous knowledge of spoken Tibetan. The English translations follow the Tibetan as closely as possible in order to help students understand both its meaning and form.

This book is written in a style which is completely different from the old traditional method. Moreover, it had been entirely based upon the modern colloquial grammatical rules, keeping in view the present requirements of the students. It is my hope that this method will truly benefit students and help them to learn both spoken and literary Tibetan. I would welcome any suggestion or comments in order to improve this book.

I would like to take this opportunity to express my sincere thanks to all of my friends who have assisted and encouraged me to write this book. Special thanks go to Mr. Gyatsho Tshering, Director of Library of Tibetan Works and Archives for reviewing the text. Also to Mr. Losang Dhonden,a Tibetan language research officer at LTWA for revising the entire Tibetan section and to Miss Kate Roddick from Britain, presently engaged in Tibetan Medical research for revising the English section.

Tashi Daknewa.

CONTENTS

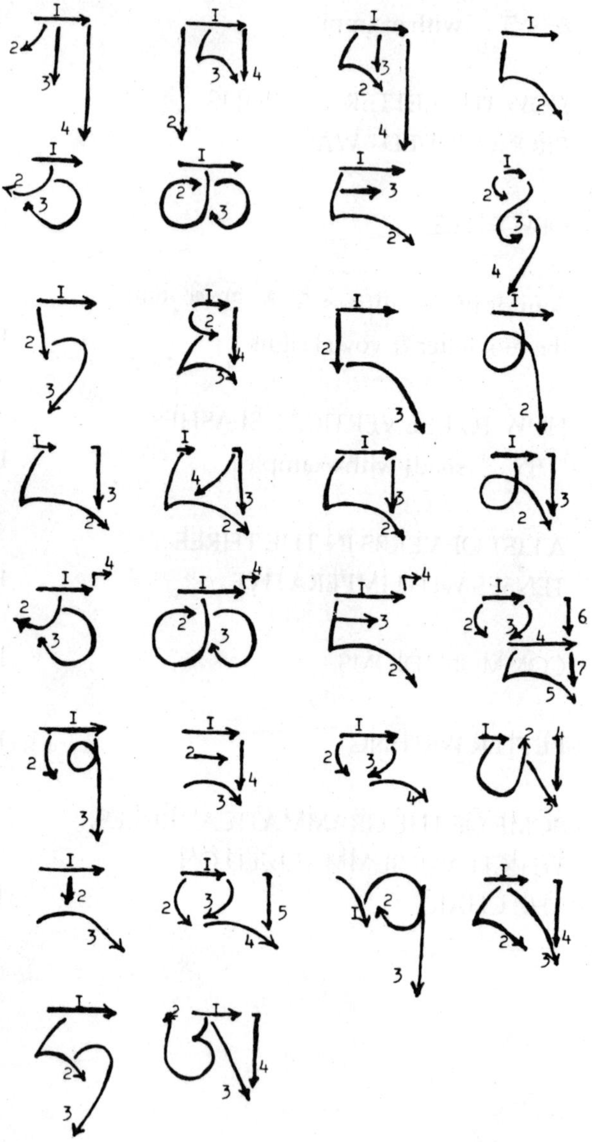

བོད་ཡིག་ཀ་ཁའི་ངོ་སྤྲོད།

Introduction of Tibetan alphabet:

The Tibetan alphabet consists of thirty consonants. They are called གསལ་བྱེད་ (sä:-ch ' e:) or ཀ་ལི་ (Ka-li). The thirty consonants are divided into seven and half groups. Each group consists of four consonants.

Thirty consonants with Romanization transliteration:

ཀ་	ཁ་	ག་	ང་	ཅ་	ཆ་	ཇ་	ཉ་
KA	KHA	GA	NGA	CA	CHA	JA	NYA
ཏ་	ཐ་	ད་	ན་	པ་	ཕ་	བ་	མ་
TA	THA	DA	NA	PA	PHA	BA	MA
ཙ་	ཚ་	ཛ་	ཝ་	ཞ་	ཟ་	འ་	ཡ་
TSA	TSHA	DZA	WA	ZHA	ZA	'A	YA
ར་	ལ་	ཤ་	ས་	ཧ་	ཨ་		
RA	LA	SHA	SA	HA	A		

དབྱངས་བཞི།

The four Vowels:

The four vowels are i, u, e & o. They are called དབྱངས་ (ȳang) or ཨཱ་ལི་ (a-li).

The four vowel signs:

[the four vowel signs with sounds]

" ི " ཨི་ = i

" ུ " ཨུ་ = u

" ེ " ཨེ་ = e

" ོ " ཨོ་ = o

Names of the four vowel signs:

" ི " The name of this sign is called གི་གུ་ (k'i-k'u)

" ུ " The name of this sign is called ཞབས་ཀྱུ་ (shab-kyu)

" ེ " The name of this sign is called འགྲེང་པོ་ (ḍeng-po)

" ོ " The name of this sign is called ན་རོ་ (Na-rō)

The unwritten vowel ཨ་ (a) is presumed in all the 29 consonants. It is said that without ཨ་ (a) the consonants would be སྲོག་མེད་ which means lifeless.

མགོ་ཅན་གསུམ།

Three types of Superscribed or Surmounting letters:

1. ར་མགོ་ (Ra-go)
2. ལ་མགོ་ (La-go)
3. ས་མགོ་ (Sa-go)

ར་མགོ་བཅུ་གཉིས་ནི། *(12 Ra-gos)*

རྐ་ རྒ་ རྔ་ རྗ་ རྙ་ རྟ་ རྡ་ རྣ་
རྦ་ རྨ་ རྩ་ རྫ་

ལ་མགོ་བཅུ་ནི། *(10 La-gos)*

ལྐ་ ལྒ་ ལྔ་ ལྕ་ ལྗ་ ལྟ་ ལྡ་ ལྤ་
ལྦ་ ལྷ་

ས་མགོ་བཅུ་གཅིག། *(11 Sa-gos)*

སྐ་ སྒ་ སྔ་ སྙ་ སྟ་ སྡ་ སྣ་ སྤ་
སྦ་ སྨ་ སྩ་

འདོགས་ཅན་བཞི།

Four types of Subjoined letters:

1. ཡ་བཏགས་ (ya-ta) ◌ྱ
2. ར་བཏགས་ (ra-ta) ◌ྲ
3. ལ་བཏགས་ (la-ta) ◌ླ
4. ཝ་སུར་ (wa-sur) ◌ྭ

ཡ་བཏགས་བརྒྱད་ནི། *(8 Ya–tas)*

ཀྱ་ ཁྱ་ གྱ་ པྱ་ ཕྱ་ བྱ་ མྱ་ ཧྱ་

ར་བཏགས་བཅུ་གསུམ་ནི། *(13 Ra-tas)*

ཀྲ་ ཁྲ་ གྲ་ ཏྲ་ ཐྲ་ དྲ་ ནྲ་ པྲ་
ཕྲ་ བྲ་ མྲ་ སྲ་ ཧྲ་

ལ་བཏགས་དྲུག་ནི། *(6 La-tas)*

ཀླ་ གླ་ བླ་ ཟླ་ སླ་ རླ་

ཝ་སུར་བཅུ་གསུམ་ནི། *(13 Wa-surs)*

ཀྭ་ ཁྭ་ གྭ ཉྭ་ དྭ་ ཙྭ་ ཚྭ་ ཞྭ་
ཟྭ་ རྭ་ ལྭ་ ཤྭ་ ཧྭ་

ལེགས་སྦྱར་གྱི་ཡི་གེ་ཁག
The Tibetanised Sanskrit letters:

ལོག་ཡིག་དྲུག (*Six reverse letters*)

ཊ་ ཋ་ ཌ་ ཎ་ ཥ་ ཀྵཿ

མཐུག་པོ་ལྔ། (*Five thick letters* or *Five heavy sounding letters*)

གྷ་ ཌྷ་ བྷ་ ཛྷ་ དྷ་

སྔོན་འཇུག་ལྔ། **Five prefixes**

ག་ ད་ བ་ མ་ འ་

Examples:

1. གཡག་ "Yak"
   *
   འདི་གཡག་རེད། This is a Yak.
2. དཀར་པོ་ "white"
   *
   གཡག་འདི་དཀར་པོ་རེད། This yak is white.
3. བཟོ་ "to make"
   *
   ང་བག་ལེབ་བཟོ་གི་ཡོད། I am making bread.

4. སྨྱོ་ "head"

གཡག་མགོ་ཆེན་པོ་ཡོག་རེད།

The head of the yak is big.

5. འདི་ "this"

འདི་འབྲིའི་མར་རེད།

This is yak butter. *

རྗེས་འཇུག་བཅུ། Ten Suffixes

ག་ ང་ ད་ ན་ བ་ མ་ འ་ ར་
ལ་ ས་

Examples:

1. ཡག་པོ་ "good"

དེབ་འདི་ཡག་པོ་འདུག

This book is good.

2. ངང་པ་ "duck"

ང་ངང་པ་ལ་དགའ་པོ་ཡོད།

I like duck.

3. ཐོད་དེ "completely"

ངས་ཐོད་དེ་རྗེད་ཤག

I have forgotten completely. or I forgot (it) completely.

---

* འབྲི་ = female yak.

4. ཉན་ "Listen"

ང་རླུང་འཕྲིན་ཉན་གྱི་ཡོད། — I am listening to the radio.

5. ཐོབ། "to win/get"

ཁོང་ཚོ་ལ་རྩེད་མོ་ཐོབ་སོང་། — They won the match/game.

6. འཇམ་པོ། "soft"

བལ་འདི་འཇམ་པོ་ཞི་དྲག་འདུག — This wool is very soft.

7. ནམ་མཁའ། "sky"

ནམ་མཁའ་ལ་སྤྲིན་པ་འདུག — There are clouds in the sky.

8. ཆར་པ། "rain"

དེ་རིང་ཆར་པ་རྒྱག་གི་འདུག — Today it's raining.

9. གལ་ཆེན་པོ། "important"

ལས་ཀ་འདི་གལ་ཆེན་པོ་རེད། — This work is important.

10. མཁས་པ། "scholar"

ཁོང་མི་མཁས་པ་ཞིག་རེད། — He is a scholar.

ཡང་འཇུག་གཉིས། **Two Post-Suffixes**

ད་ & ས་

Examples:

1. ཕྱིནད། "went"

ང་བོད་ལ་ཕྱིནད་པ་ཡིན། I went to Tibet.

2. གངས་རི། "snow mountain"

བོད་ལ་གངས་རི་མང་པོ་ཡོག་རེད། There are many snow mountians in Tibet.

Note: The post suffix ད (da) is not used anymore but it is important to know the rule.

Some important notes:

1. A single consonant is always a root letter.

Examples:

ཁ་	ང་	ཆ་	ཇ་	ཉ་	ད་	ན་
པ་	ཕ་	ས་ etc.				

2. All the three types of superscribed consonants, four types of subjoined letters, five heavy sounding letters, the Tibetanised Sanskrit letters and vowel signs are used only in the root letter.

Examples:

ཀ་ ཕྱ་ སྟ་ ཀྱ་ གྲ་ ཟླ་ སྒྲ་

ི ུ etc.

3. When two consonants are together, the first consonant is the root letter and the second is the suffix.

Examples:

ཁང་ དད་ ནང་ and དང་ etc.

4. When three consonants are together, the first consonant is the prefix, the second is the root letter, the third is the suffix.

Examples:

གཡག་ གནས་ མཁས་ གདན་ etc.

5. When four consonants are together, the first consonant is the prefix, the second is the root letter, the third is the suffix and the last is the post-suffix.

Examples:

མདངས་ བཙགས་ གདམས་ etc.

The following *thirty one exceptions* with the first consonant as the root letter:

1.	ཁམས་	2.	གངས་	3.	ཉམས་	4.	ཐགས་
5.	ཐབས་	6.	ཐམས་	7.	ནགས་	8.	ནངས་
9.	ནམས་	10.	པགས་	11.	ཚགས་	12.	ཚངས་
13.	ཚབས་	14.	ཕངས་	15.	བངས་	16.	བབས་
17.	བགས་	18.	ཞབས་	19.	ཞགས་	20.	ཟངས་
21.	ཟབས་	22.	ཡངས་	23.	ཡམས་	24.	རབས་
25.	རགས་	26.	རངས་	27.	ལངས་	28.	ལགས་
29.	ཤགས་	30.	ཤངས་	31.	སངས་		

ཚིག་སྒྲུབ། (The sentence)

The construction of a Tibetan sentence is very different from English but in some way it is very close to Hindi, Japanese and the Korean language.

The proper order of framing a Tibetan sentence in general:

Firstly place the *Subject* then the *Noun* & finally the *Verb*

Examples:

1. ང་ཟླ་བ་ཡིན། I am Dawa.
   I–Dawa–is
2. ཁོང་སྒྲོལ་མ་ལགས་རེད།
   She is Dolma la.
3. འདི་དེབ་རེད།
   This is (a) book.
4. འདི་ཚོ་སྨྱུ་གུ་རེད།
   These are pens.
5. དེ་གྲྭ་པ་རེད།
   That is (a) monk.

6. དེ་ཚོ་གཡག་རེད།

Those are Yaks.

The following Tibetan sentences indicate the use of tense. The pattern is the same, but the verb compliment follows after the main verb.

Subject – Noun – Main verb – Verb compliment

Examples:

1. ང་དེབ་ཀློག་གི་ཡོད།

I–book–read–present tense.

I am reading (a) book.

2. ཁྱེད་རང་ཡི་གེ་འབྲི་གི་འདུག

You are writing (a) letter. (*Present*)

3. ཁོང་ལྡི་ལི་ལ་ཕེབས་སོང་།

He/she went to Delhi. (*Past*)

4. ང་ཚོ་འཆམ་འཆམ་ལ་འགྲོ་གི་ཡིན།

We will go for a walk. (*Future*)

Note: Change the sentences into nagative by adding "མ" (ma) before the main verb.

Thus:

1. འདི་ཁང་པ་མ་རེད། This is not (a) house.
2. འདི་ཚོ་ཚ་ལུ་མ་མ་རེད། These are not oranges.
3. ཁོང་ངའི་བུ་མ་རེད། He is not my son.

མིང་ཚིག (The noun)

Study the list of Common Nouns.

A) སྤྱི་མིང་ (common noun)

A name which does not point out any particular person or thing, but is common to all persons, places or things. This is called a common noun.

Thus:

1. གང་ཟག་གི་མིང་། (Persons)

དགེ་རྒན།	teacher
ཨ་ཁུ།	uncle
ཨ་ནེ།	aunt
མོ་ཊ་གཏོང་མཁན།	driver
(ཁ་ལོ་བ་)	
ཨེམ་ཆི།	doctor
ནར་སི།	nurse
སོའི་ཨེམ་ཆི།	dentist
དམག་མི།	soldier
ཞིང་པ།	farmer
བུ།	boy

2. ས་ཆའི་མིང་། (Places)

Examples:

གླིང་ག	park
ཐབ་ཚང་།	kitchen
སྲིན་གཟིགས་ཁང་།	zoo
སྨན་ཁང་།	hospital

ཐོག	roof
ལམ།	street/way
དགོན་པ།	monastery
ལྷ་ཁང་།	temple
འགྲེམས་འདོན་ཁང་།	museum

3. སེམས་ཅན་གྱི་མིང་། (Animals)

Examples:

རྟ།	horse
སྟག	tiger
སེང་གེ	lion
རི་བོང་།	rabbit
ཙེ་ཙེ།	mouse
སྤྲེའུ།	monkey
ཕུག་རོན།	pigeon
རྨ་བྱ།	peacock
དུག་སྦྲང་།	mosquito
ཞི་མི།	cat

4. དངོས་པོའི་མིང་། (Things)

Examples:

སྐུད་པ།	thread
ཁབ།	needle
ལྷམ།	shoe
ཐ་མག	cigarettes
མེ་འཁོར།	train
མོ་ཊ།	bus/car/jeep
ཅི་ནི་ཀ་ར།	sugar
དར་ཆ།	flag
དེབ།	book

B) ཁྱད་སྤྱག་གི་མིང་། (Proper noun)

A name which belongs to a particular person, place or things is called a proper noun.

Examples:

ལྷ་ས།	Lhasa (*The capital of Tibet*)
ཇོ་ཁང་།	Jo-khang
སེ་ར།	Sera (*name of a monastery*)

རྒྱ་གར།	India
བལ་ཡུལ།	Nepal
ཟླ་བ།	Dawa
སྒྲོལ་མ།	Dolma
ཚེ་རིང་།	Tsering

C) ཤེས་འཚོར་གྱི་མིང་། (Abstract noun)

A name given to some state, quality of feeling that we can only think of is called an Abstract noun.

Examples:

སེམས་ཤུགས།	courage
ན་ཚ།	pain
ཚོར་བ།	feeling
བཀའ་དྲིན།	kindness/gratitude

D) ཚོགས་མིང་། (Collective noun)

A name given to a collection of persons or things is called a Collective noun.

Examples:

འཚང་ག།	crowd
ཁྱུ།	flock
དམག་མི།	army/soldiers
ཚག་པ།	bunch

བྱ་ཚིག (The verb)

In Tibetan language a verb is divided into two forms.

1. སྤྱིར་བཏང་ (Ordinary form or non–honorific)
2. ཞེ་ས་ (honorific)

Study the list of the verbs:

Non–honorific		Honorific
འགྲོ་	to go	ཕེབས་
འཐུང་	to drink	མཆོད་
ཉན་	to listen	གསན་
ཉོ་	to buy	སྐུས་གཟིགས་གནང་
མཐོང་	to see	གཟིགས་
ཉལ་	to sleep	གཟིམ་
ཐུག་	to meet	མཇལ་
མངག་	to order	བཀའ་མངགས་
སྡོད་	to sit/stay/live	བཞུགས་
ཚོང་	to sell	སྐུས་ཚོང་གནང་
ལང་	to get up	བཞེངས་
སྒྱུར་	to translate	སྒྱུར་གནང་
ངུ་	to cry	ཐུམ་
འབྲི་	to write	འབྲི་གནང་

ཀློག་ to read ལྗགས་ཀློག་

The above mentioned verbs can be illustrated by the following examples:

1. ང་ལྡི་ལི་ལ་འགྲོ་གི་ཡིན།

   I will go to Delhi.

2. ཁྱེད་རང་སྒྲུང་དེབ་ཀློག་གནང་གི་འདུག

   You are reading (a) story book.

3. ཟླ་འོད་ལགས་ཤུག་དེབ་སྒྲུས་གཟིགས་གནང་གི་འདུག

   Dawoe is purchasing (a) book.

4. ཁོང་གིས་དེབ་ཞིག་བསྒྱུར་གནང་གི་རེད།

   He/She will translate a book.

5. ངས་དེབ་ཁ་ཤས་མངགས་པ་ཡིན།

   I have ordered some books.

མིང་གི་ཁྱད་ཆོས། (The Adjective)

A word which describes something is called an adjec

Examples:

1. ཆེན་པོ་ big
2. ཆུང་ཆུང་ small
3. མང་པོ་ many
4. ཉུང་ཉུང་ few/some
5. ཡག་པོ་ good

མིང་གི་ཁྱད་ཆོས་སྐྱར་ཆིག་ཁྱད་རིམ་སྟོན་པ།

Comparisons of Adjectives

1. The adjective ཤུགས་ཆེན་པོ་(strong) is said to be in the Positive Degree. It simply denotes the existence of some quality of a thing or person we speak about. It is used when no comparison is made.

   ཚེ་རིང་ཤུགས་ཆེན་པོ་ཡོག་རེད་/ འདུག

   Tsering is strong.

2. The adjective ཤུགས་ཆེ་བ་(stronger) is said to be in the Comparative Degree. It denotes a higher

degree of the quality than the positive. It is used when two persons or things are compared.

ཚེ་རིང་ལས་དོན་གྲུབ་ཤུགས་ཆེ་བ་ཡོག་རེད། འདུག

Dhondup is stronger than Tsering.

3. The adjective ཤུགས་ཆེ་ཤོས་ (strongest) is said to be in the Superlative Degree. It denotes the higher degree of the quality. It is used when more than two persons or things are compared.

པ་སངས་ཤུགས་ཆེ་ཤོས་ཡོག་རེད། འདུག

Pasang is the strongest.

Formation of Comparison and Superlative

a) Most adjectives form their comparative degree by adding བ་ (wa) and their superlative by adding ཤོས་ to the positive in the following comparisons.

མིང་ཚིག་ཁྱད་ཆོས་ Positive	ཁྱད་ཆོས་ ཁྱད་འཕར་ Comparative	ཁྱད་ཆོས་ ཀུན་ལས་འཕགས་པ་ Superlative
ཆེན་པོ་	ཆེ་བ་	ཆེ་ཤོས་
big	biggger	biggest

ཚ་པོ་	ཚ་བ་	ཚ་ཤོས་
hot	hoter	hotest
ཕྱི་པོ་	ཕྱི་བ་	ཕྱི་ཤོས་
late	later	latest
དལ་པོ་	དལ་བ་	དལ་ཤོས་
slow	slower	slowest
སྔ་པོ་	སྔ་བ	སྔ་ཤོས་
early	earlier	earliest
དགའ་པོ་	དགའ་བ་	དགའ་ཤོས་
happy	happier	happiest
སྐྱོ་པོ་	སྐྱོ་བ་	སྐྱོ་ཤོས་
poor	poorer	poorest
ལྗིད་པོ་	ལྗིད་པ་	ལྗིད་ཤོས་
heavy	heavier	heavest
སྙིང་རྗེ་པོ་	སྙིང་རྗེ་བ་	སྙིང་རྗེ་ཤོས་
pretty	prettier	prettiest
ཤུགས་ཆེན་པོ་	ཤུགས་ཆེ་བ་	ཤུགས་ཆེ་ཤོས་
strong	stronger	strongest

B) In some cases the adjective form their comparative degree by adding བ་ (wa) in written form and by adding ང་(nga) or ར་(ra) in the spoken language. The superlative by adding ཤོས་ to the positive in the following comparisons.

མིང་གི་ཁྱད་ཆོས་ Positive	ཁྱད་ཆོས་ ཁྱད་འཕར་ Comparative	ཁྱད་ཆོས་ ཀུན་ལས་འཕགས་པ་ Superlative
ཆུང་ཆུང	ཆུང་བ་/ ང་	ཆུང་ཤོས་
small	smaller	smallest
གསར་པ་	གསར་བ་/ ར་	གསར་ཤོས་
new	newer	newest
མངར་མོ་	མངར་བ་/ ར་	མངར་ཤོས་
sweet	sweeter	sweetest
གྲང་མོ་	གྲང་བ་/ ང་	གྲང་ཤོས་
cold	colder	coldest
མང་པོ་	མང་བ་/ ང་	མང་ཤོས་
many	more	most
ཉུང་ཉུང་	ཉུང་བ་/ ང་	ཉུང་ཤོས་

few	fewer	fewest
རིང་པོ་	རིང་བ་/ ང་	རིང་ཤོས་
long/tall	longer/taller	longest/tallest
ཡང་པོ་	ཡང་བ་/ ང་	ཡང་ཤོས་
light	lighter	lightest
ཐག་རིང་པོ་	ཐག་རིང་བ་/ ང་	ཐག་རིང་ཤོས་
far	further	furthest
ཉིང་པ་	ཉིང་བ་/ ང་	ཉིང་ཤོས་
old	older	oldest
བཟང་པོ་	བཟང་བ་/ ང་	བཟང་ཤོས་
noble	nobler	noblest

C) In some cases the adjective form their comparative degree by adding པ་ (pa) in written form and by adding ག་(ga) in the spoken language and their superlative by adding ཤོས་ to the positive

མིང་གི་ཁྱད་ཆོས་ Positive	ཁྱད་ཆོས་ ཁྱད་འཕར་ Comparative	ཁྱད་ཆོས་ ཀུན་ལས་འཕགས་པ་ Superlative
ཡག་པོ་ good	ཡག་པ་/ ག་ better	ཡག་ཤོས་ best
མཐུག་པོ་ thick	མཐུག་པ་/ ག་ thicker	མཐུག་ཤོས་ thickest
རྒྱགས་པ་ fat	རྒྱགས་པ་/ ག་ fatter	རྒྱགས་ཤོས་ fattest
མགྱོགས་པོ་ fast	མགྱོགས་པ་/ ག་ faster	མགྱོགས་ཤོས་ fastest
སྡུག་པོ་ bad	སྡུག་པ་/ ག་ worse	སྡུག་ཤོས་ worst
ཕྱུག་པོ་ rich	ཕྱུག་པ་/ ག་ richer	ཕྱུག་ཤོས་ richest

D) In some cases the adjective form their comparative degree by adding པ་ (pa) and the superlative degree is the same as mentioned above.

Thus:

མིང་གི་ཁྱད་ཆོས་	ཁྱད་ཆོས་ ཁྱད་འཕར་	ཁྱད་ཆོས་ ཀུན་ལས་འཕགས་པ་
Positive	Comparative	Superlative
མཛེས་པོ་ beautiful	མཛེས་པ་ more beautiful	མཛེས་ཤོས་ most beautiful
གཞོན་གཞོན་ young	གཞོན་པ་ younger	གཞོན་ཤོས་ youngest
སྐམ་པོ་ thin	སྐམ་པ་ thinner	སྐམ་ཤོས་ thinnest [of person only]
ངན་པོ་ bad	ངན་པ་ worse	ངན་ཤོས worst
སྲབ་པོ་ thin	སྲབ་པ་ thinner	སྲབ་ཤོས་ thinnest [of things only]

རྒྱས་པོ་	རྒྱས་པ་	རྒྱས་ཤོས་
detailed	more detailed	most detailed
བསྡུས་པོ་	བསྡུས་པ་	བསྡུས་ཤོས་
brief	briefer	briefest

མིང་ཚབ། (The Pronoun: kinds of pronouns)

The words ཁོང་ (he/she), ཁོང་ཚོ་ (they), ཁྱེད་རང་ (you), and ཁྱེད་རང་ཚོ་ (you pl.) are used instead of names or (nouns). These are known as Pronouns.

གང་ཟག་གི་མིང་ཚབ།

Personal Pronouns:

The pronouns which indicate the names of persons or things. Such pronouns are called personal pronouns.

གང་ཟག་དང་པོའི་མིང་ཚབ།

Pronouns of the first person:

The pronouns ང་ (I), ང་ལ་ (me) , ང་ཚོ་ (we), ང་ཚོ་ལ་ (us) refer to the person speaking. They are , therefore, said to be pronouns of the first person.

Examples:

1. ང་ཉིན་ལྟར་སློབ་གྲྭར་འགྲོ་གི་ཡོད།

   I go to school daily.

2. བསྟན་འཛིན་གྱིས་ང་ལ་སྨྱུ་གུ་གཅིག་སྤྲད་བྱུང་།

   Tenzin gave me a pen.

3. ང་ཚོ་འཛིན་གྲྭ་གཅིག་པ་ཡིན།

   We are in the same class.

4. ང་ཚོ་ལ་རྒན་ལགས་ཀྱིས་མཉེས་པོ་གནང་གི་ཡོག་རེད།

   The teacher likes us.

གང་ཟག་གཉིས་པའི་མིང་ཚབ།

Pronouns of the second person:

The pronouns ཁྱེད་རང་ (you singular) and ཁྱེད་རང་ཚོ་ (you plural) refer to the person spoken to. They are, therefore, said to be pronouns of the second person.

Examples:

1. ཁྱེད་རང་བུ་ཡག་པོ་ཞིག་རེད།

   You are a good boy.

2. ངས་ཁྱེད་རང་ཚོ་ལ་ཕྱི་པོ་མ་ཡོང་ལབ་པ་ཡིན།

I told you not to come late.

3. ཁྱེད་རང་ཁའི་ས་ག་པར་ཕྱིན་པ།

Where did you go yesterday?

གང་ཟག་གསུམ་པའི་མིང་ཚབ།

Pronouns of the third person:

The pronouns ཁོ་(he), མོ (she), ཁོང་ (he / she) ཁོང་གི་ (his/her), ཁོང་ཚོ་ (they), ཁོང་ཚོ་ལ་(them) refer to the person spoken of. They are, therefore, said to be pronouns of the third person.

Examples:

1. ཁོང་མི་ཡག་པོ་འདུག

He is (a) good man.

2. ཁོང་ལ་འདིར་མ་ཕེབས་གསུང་རོགས།

Tell him not to come here.

3. ཁོང་གིས་གཞས་ཡག་པོ་གཏོང་ཐུབ་ཀྱི་ཡོག་རེད།

She / he can sing well.

4. ཁོང་ལ་སང་ཉིན་གཞས་གཅིག་གཏོང་རོགས་གསུང་རོགས།

Please tell her/him to sing a song for tomorrow.

5. ཁོང་ཚོ་བོད་ལ་ཕེབས་པ་རེད།

They went to Tibet.

6. དེབ་འདི་ཁོང་ཚོ་ལ་གནང་རོགས་གནང་།

Please give this book to them.

དམིགས་སྟོན་དགར་བའི་མིང་ཚབ།

Demonstrative Pronouns:

The demonstrative pronouns འདི་(this), དེ་(that), འདི་ཚོ་(these) and དེ་ཚོ་ (those) are used to point out the object or objects to which they refer. They are called demonstrative pronouns.

Examples:

1. འདི་ཞི་མི་རེད།

This is (a) cat.

2. འདི་ཚོ་ཀུ་ཤུ་རེད།

These are apples.

3. དེ་ཚོ་ཁྱེད་རང་གི་ཁང་པ་རེད།

Those are your houses.

བྱེད་པ་པོ་དང་འབྲེལ་བའི་མིང་ཚབ།

Reflexive Pronouns:

The demonstrative ང་རང་རང་ (myself), ང་ཚོ་རང་ (ourselves), ཁྱེད་རང་རང་ (yourself), ཁྱེད་རང་ཚོ་རང་ (yourselves) ཁོང་རང་རང་ (himself/herself) and ཁོང་ཚོ་རང་ (themselves) when used as the object of a verb are called Reflexive Pronouns.

Examples:

1. ང་རང་རང་ལ་སྐྱོན་བརྗོད་བྱས་པ་ཡིན།

I have criticized myself.

2. ཁྱེད་རང་གིས་ཁྱེད་རང་རང་ལ་སྐྱོན་བརྗོད་གནང་སོང་།

You have criticized yourself.

3. ཁོང་གིས་ཁོང་རང་རང་ལ་སྐྱོན་བརྗོད་གནང་སོང་།

He/ she has criticized himself or herself.

4. ང་ཚོས་ང་ཚོ་རང་ལ་སྐྱོན་བརྗོད་བྱས་པ་ཡིན།

We have criticized ourselves.

5. ཁྱེད་རང་ཚོས་ཁྱེད་རང་ཚོ་རང་ལ་སྐྱོན་བརྗོད་གནང་སོང་།

You (plural) have criticized yourselves.

6. ཁོང་ཚོས་ཁོང་ཚོ་རང་ལ་སྐྱོན་བརྗོད་གནང་སོང་།

They have criticized themselves.

འདྲི་ཚིག་གི་མིང་ཚབ།

Interrogative Pronouns:

The pronouns སུ་ (who), སུ་ལ་ (whom),ག་གི་ (which) སུའི་ (whose) ག་རེ་ (what) are used for asking questions. They are, therefore, called Interrogative pronouns.

Examples:

1. དེར་སུ་འདུག

Who is there?

2. ཁྱེད་རང་གི་ཁང་པ་ག་གི་རེད།

Which is your house?

3. དེབ་འདི་སུའི་རེད།

whose book is this?

4. ཁྱེད་རང་ལ་ག་རེ་དགོས་ཀྱི་འདུག

What do you want?

5. དེབ་འདི་སུ་ལ་གནང་གི་ཡིན།

To whom will this book be given?

ལ་དོན།

The Preposition

In literary form སུ་ ཏུ་ དུ་ རུ་ and ན་ have the function of to, in, into, for, and at. These grammatical rules are summarized on the chart given in the end of this book.
[see page No. 181]

The above mentioned སུ་ ཏུ་ དུ་ རུ་ and ན་ are replaced by ར་ and ལ་ commonly used in the colloquial Tibetan after any suffix, and possesing the signification of all the above prepositions.

Examples:

1. ང་བོད་ལ་འགྲོ་གི་ཡིན།

   I will go to Tibet.

2. བོད་ལ་གཡག་ཡོག་རེད།

   There are yaks in Tibet.

3. ང་ལྷ་སར་ཕྱིན་པ་ཡིན།

   I went to Lhasa.

4. ང་དྷ་རམ་ས་ལར་འགྲོ་གི་ཡིན།

I will go to Dharamsala.

5. ང་ཚོ་དཔེ་མཛོད་ཁང་ལ་འགྲོ་གི་ཡིན།

We will go to the Library.

6. ཛན་པ་འདི་ཁྱེད་རང་ལ་ཡིན།

This gift is for you.

7. ང་ལྷ་ཁང་གི་ནང་ལ་འགྲོ་གི་ཡིན།

I will go into the temple.

Study the list of prepositions and use them in the sentences.

1.	ནང་ལ་	in
2.	སྒང་ལ་	on
3.	འོག་ལ་	under
4.	འཁྲིས་ལ་	near
5.	ཉེ་འགྲམ་	beside
6.	དེའི་སྒང་ལ་	above
7.	མདུན་ལ་	infront of

Examples:

1. དེབ་སྒམ་ནང་ལ་ཡོད།

The book is in the box.

2. དེབ་སྒམ་གྱི་སྟེང་ལ་ཡོད།

The book is on the box.

3. དེབ་སྒམ་གྱི་འོག་ལ་ཡོད།

The book is under the box.

4. དེབ་སྒམ་གྱི་འཁྲིས་ལ་ཡོད།

The book is near the box.

5. དེབ་སྒམ་གྱི་ཉེ་འགྲམ་ལ་ཡོད།

The book is beside the box.

6. དེབ་སྒམ་དེའི་སྟེང་ལ་ཡོད།

The book is above the box.

7. དེབ་སྒམ་གྱི་མདུན་ལ་ཡོད།

The book is in front of the box.

The word " སྟེང་ལ་ " " འོག་ལ་ " " ཉེ་འགྲམ་ལ་ "

"དེའི་སྟེངལ་" " མདུན་ལ་ " show the relation in which

the book stands to the box.

ཚིག་ཕྲད་མིང་ཚབ་མཉམ་དུ་སྦྱར་བ།

The preposition used with pronouns:

སྟེང་ལ་	above
རྗེས་ལ་ /རྒྱབ་ལ་	behind
མཉམ་དུ་	with / together
ཉེ་འགྲམ་ལ་	beside

Examples:

1. ང་ཚོའི་སྟེང་ལ་གནམ་གྲུ་འདུག

   The aeroplane is above us.

2. ང་ཁྱེད་རང་མཉམ་དུ་འགྲོ་གི་ཡིན།

   I will go with you.

3. ཕྲུ་གུས་ཁོང་གི་རྗེས་ལ་གོམ་པ་བརྒྱབས་སོང་།

   The children walked behind him.

4. ཁོང་ངའི་ཉེ་འགྲམ་ལ་བཞུགས་སོང་།

   He/she sat beside me.

བྱ་བའི་ཁྱད་ཆིག

The Adverb

Tibetan adverbs are divided into four groups:

བྱ་བའི་ཚུལ་སྟོན་པའི་ཁྱད་ཚོས།

Adverbs of manner

ག་ལེ་ག་ལེར་	slowly
མགྱོགས་པོ་	fast
དགའ་པོ་བྱས་ནས་	happily

Examples:

1. སྤོའི་ལགས་རྒན་ཁོག་དེས་གོམ་པ་ག་ལེ་ག་ལེར་བརྒྱབས་སོང་

   The old man walked slowly.

2. བུ་དེ་མགྱོགས་པོ་རྒྱུགས་ཀྱི་འདུག

   The boy runs fast.

3. ཕྲུ་གུ་ཚོས་སྐྱིད་པོ་བྱས་རྩེད་མོ་རྩེས་སོང་།

   The children played happily.

The adverb ག་ལེ་ག་ལེར་ (slowly), མགྱོགས་པོ་(fast) and སྐྱིད་པོ་བྱས་ནས་(happily) add something to the meaning of of the verbs གོམ་པ་བརྒྱབས་ (walked) རྒྱུགས་ (runs) and རྩེད་མོ་རྩེས་ (played). They tell us how the action is done. These adverbs which show the manner in which some action is done, are called Adverbs of manner.

བྱ་བའི་དུས་སྟོན་པའི་ཁྱད་ཆོས།

Adverbs of time

ཁ་ས་	yesterday
མཚམས་མཚམས་ལ་	occasionally
ཕྱི་པོ་	late
སང་ཉིན་	tomorrow

Examples:

1. སྒྲོལ་མ་ལགས་ཁ་ས་ཕེབས་སོང་།

   Dolına came yesterday.

2. ཁོང་བོད་ལ་མཚམས་མཚམས་ལ་འགྲོ་གི་རེད།

   He will go to Tibet occassionally.

3. ཁོང་ནང་ལ་ཕྱི་པོ་ཡོང་གི་རེད།

   He/she comes home late.

4. ཁོང་སང་ཉིན་འབྱོར་གྱི་རེད།

   He/she will arrive tomorrow.

The word ཁ་སང་ (yesterday), མཚམས་མཚམས་ (occasionally), ཕྱི་པོ་ (late) and སང་ཉིན་ (tomorrow) add something to the meaning of the verbs ཕེབས་སོང་ (came), འགྲོ་གི་རེད་ (will go) ཡོང་གི་ཡོག་རེད་ (comes) and འབྱོར་ (arrive). They tell us when the action is done.

Such adverbs are called Adverbs of time.

བྱ་བའི་ཡུལ་སྟོན་པའི་ཁྱད་ཆོས།

Adverbs of place:

སྟེང་ལ་	above
ཡར་	up
འདིར་ (འདའི་)	here
ཕྱི་ལོགས་ལ་	outside

Examples:

1. ངས་ཡར་བལྟས་པ་ཡིན།

   I looked up.

2. ཁོང་འདིར་བཞུགས་ཀྱི་ཡོག་རེད།

   He/she lives here.

3. ཁོང་ཚོ་ཕྱི་ལོགས་ལ་ཕེབས་སོང་།

   They went outside.

The words ཡར་ (up) འདིར་ (here) ཕྱི་ལོགས་ལ་ (outside) add something to the meaning of the verbs བལྟས་ (looked), བཞུགས་ཀྱི་ཡོག་རེད་ (lives) and ཕེབས་སོང་ (went). They tell us where the action takes place. Such adverbs are called Adverbs of place.

བྱ་བའི་ཁྱད་རིམ་སྟོན་པའི་ཁྱད་ཚོས།

Adverbs of degree:

ཞེ་དྲག་	very
ཧ་ལམ་	almost
ཧ་ཅང་	too / extremely

Examples:

1. ལྡུམ་ར་འདི་ཞེ་དྲག་སྙིང་རྗེ་པོ་འདུག

   This garden is very beautiful.

2. ཚ་ལུ་མ་འདི་ཚོ་ཧ་ལམ་འཚོས་འདུག

   These oranges are almost ripe.

3. ལེའུ་འདི་ཧ་ཅང་རིང་པོ་འདུག

   This chapter is too long.

The adverbs " ཞི་དྲག་" (very) " ཏ་ལམ་" (almost) and " ཏ་ཙང་" (extremely) which show in what degree or to what extent something is done. These are called Adverbs of degree.

བྱ་བའི་ཚིག་གྲོགས་ཀྱི་དུས་གསུམ་རྣམ་གཞག

Verb complements / Different Tense endings :

In Tibetan sentences the different tense verb endings denote the action in the present, past and future. Thus, there are three main tense endings or verb complements for the first person. i.e ང་ (I) and ང་ཚོ་(we)

གི་ཡིན། indicates the future tense (མ་འོངས་པ་)
གི་ཡོད། indicates the present tense (ད་ལྟ་བ)
པ་ཡིན། indicates the past tense (འདས་པ་)

The below mentioned three main tense endings or verb complements are for the second and third person. i.e.

ཁྱེད་རང་ (you) ཁོང་ (he /she) ཁོང་ཚོ་ (they)

གི་རེད། indicates the future tense (མ་འོངས་པ་)

གི་འདུག indicates the present tense (ད་ལྟ་བ་)

པ་རེད་/བ་རེད or སོང་། indicates the past tense (འདས་པ་)

The above mentioned eight main tense endings or verb complements are used right after the verbs in the three tenses ; such as : གཏང་(will send) future tense, གཏོང་ (send) present tense བཏང་ (sent) past tense. The verbs and verb complements are essencial for indicating the tense of a Tibetan sentence

The negative forms of the eight verb complements:

Positive		Negative	
གི་ཡིན།	(future)	གི་མིན།	(future)
གི་ཡོད།	(present)	གི་མེད།	(present)
པ་ཡིན།	(past)	མེད།	(past)
གི་རེད།	(future)	གི་མ་རེད།	(future)
གི་འདུག	(present)	གི་མི་འདུག	(present)
པ་རེད་	(past)	པ་མ་རེད།	(past)
བ་རེད།	(past)	བ་མ་རེད།	(past)
སོང་།	(past)	མ་ སོང་།	(past)

པ་རེད། བ་རེད། སོང་། are the verb complements or tense endings for the second and third persons in the past.

པ་རེད། བ་རེད། are used in a sentence in the past for the second and third persons; which indicates less certain, or in commonly known situations.

སོང་། is also used in a sentence in the past for the second and third persons; which indicate first hand visual knowledge.

In Tibetan language some verbs have the same form in the present and future tenses.

Examples:

Present tense		Future tense	Past tense
འགྲོ་	to go	འགྲོ་	ཕྱིན་
འཐུང་	to drink	འཐུང་/བཏུང་	བཏུངས་
ཉོ་	to buy	ཉོ	ཉོས་
བཟོ་	to make	བཟོ་	བཟོས་

In some cases the verbs have the same form in the present, future and past.

Examples:

Present tense		Future tense	Past tense
ཉན་	to listen	ཉན་	ཉན་
ལབ་	to tell	ལབ་	ལབ་
ཡོང་	to come	ཡོང	ཡོང
ཉལ	to sleep	ཉལ་	ཉལ་

In some cases the verbs have the different forms in the present, future and past. They are called irregular verbs.

Examples:

Present tense		Future tense	Past tense
གཏོང་	to send	གཏང	བཏང་
ཚོང	to sell	བཙོང་	བཙོངས་
སྒོམ་	to meditate	སྒོམ་	བསྒོམས་
གསོད་	to kill	གསད་	བསད་

These three tense endings or verb complements are used after the verbs in the three tenses to indicate the use of tenses.

གང་ཟག་དང་པོ། (First person: ང་ I & ང་ཚོ་ we)

གི་ཡིན། indicates the future tense (མ་འོངས་པ་)

གི་ཡོད། indicates the present tense (ད་ལྟ་བ་)

པ་ཡིན། indicates the past tense (འདས་པ་)

Verbs in the three tenses :

Present tense		Future tense	Past tense
འགྲོ་	to go	འགྲོ་	ཕྱིན་
འཐུང་	to drink	བཏུང་	བཏུངས་
ཀློག་	to read	ཀློག་ (བཀློག་)	ཀློགས་

The above mentioned verb complements and verbs in the three tenses can be illustrated by the following examples.

1. ང་འགྲོ་གི་ཡིན།

   I will go.

   ང་འགྲོ་གི་ཡོད།

   I am going.

ང་ཕྱིན་པ་ཡིན།

I went.

2. ང་ཇ་འཐུང་གི་ཡིན།

I will drink tea.

ང་ཇ་འཐུང་གི་ཡོད།

I am drinking tea.

ངས་ཇ་བཏུངས་པ་ཡིན།

I drank tea.

3. ང་ཚོ་དེབ་ཀློག་གི་ཡིན།

We will read books.

ང་ཚོ་དེབ་ཀློག་གི་ཡོད།

We are reading books.

ང་ཚོས་དེབ་ཀློགས་པ་ཡིན།

We read book.

གང་ཟག་གཉིས་པ། (Second person: ཁྱེད་རང་ you)

གི་རེད། indicates the future tense (མ་འོངས་པ་)

གི་འདུག inicates the present tense (ད་ལྟ་བ་)

པ་རེད། / སོང་། indicates the past tense (འདས་པ་)

Verbs in the three tenses :

Future tense		Present tense	Past tense
ཚོང་	to sell	བཙོང་	བཙོངས་
འབྲི་	to write / paint	འབྲི་	བྲིས་
བཟོ་	to make	བཟོ་	བཟོས་

Use the above mentioned verb complements and

verbs in the sentences.

1. ཁྱེད་རང་གིས་བཙོང་གི་རེད།

   You will sell.

   ཁྱེད་རང་ཚོང་གི་འདུག

   You are selling.

   ཁྱེད་རང་གིས་བཙོངས་པ་རེད། / སོང་།

   You sold.

2. ཁྱེད་རང་གིས་ཐང་ཀ་འབྲི་གི་རེད།

   You will paint (a) Thangka.

   ཁྱེད་རང་ཐང་ཀ་འབྲི་གི་འདུག

   You are painting (a) Thangka.

   ཁྱེད་རང་གིས་ཐང་ཀ་བྲིས་པ་རེད། / སོང་།

   You painted (a) Thangka.

3. ཁྱེད་རང་གིས་གསོལ་ཇ་བཟོ་གནང་གི་རེད།

You will make tea. (honorific)

ཁྱེད་རང་གསོལ་ཇ་བཟོ་གནང་གི་འདུག

You are making tea. (h)

ཁྱེད་རང་གིས་གསོལ་ཇ་བཟོས་གནང་པ་རེད། / སོང་།

You made tea. (h)

གང་ཟག་གསུམ་པ། (Third person: ཁོང་ he / she
ཁོང་ཚོ་ they)

གི་རེད། indicates the future tense (མ་འོངས་པ་)

གི་འདུག indicates the present tense (ད་ལྟ་བ་)

པ་རེད། / སོང་། indicates the past tense (འདས་པ་)

Verbs in the three tenses :

Present tense		Future tense	Past tense
བྱེད་	to do	བྱ་/ བྱེད་	བྱས་
ཉོ་	to buy	ཉོ་	ཉོས་
གཏོང་	to send	གཏང་	བཏང་

Examples:

1. ཁོང་གིས་ཤིང་ཏོག་ཉོ་གི་རེད།

He / she will buy fruits.

ཁོང་ཤིང་ཏོག་ཉོ་གི་འདུག

He is buying fruits.

ཁོང་གིས་ཤིང་ཏོག་ཉོས་པ་རེད། / སོང་།

He bought (some) fruits.

2. ཁོང་ཚོ་སློབ་སྦྱོང་གནང་གི་རེད།

They will study.

ཁོང་ཚོ་སློབ་སྦྱོང་གནང་གི་འདུག

They are studying.

ཁོང་ཚོས་སློབ་སྦྱོང་གནང་པ་རེད། / སོང་།

They studied.

3. ཁོང་ཚོ་གཞས་གཏང་གནང་གི་རེད།

They will sing a song.

ཁོང་ཚོ་གཞས་གཏོང་གནང་གི་འདུག

They are singing.

ཁོང་ཚོས་གཞས་བཏང་གནང་པ་རེད། / སོང་།

They sang a song.

ཚིག་སྒྲ །

Articles (A, An, The)

ཞིག་ (a / an) is used in the literary form.

ཅིག་ (a / an) is used in the colloquial form.

Examples:

Literary	Colloquial	Number
མི་ཞིག་	མི་ཅིག་	མི་གཅིག་
a man	a man	one man / person
ཚ་ལུ་མ་ཞིག་	ཚ་ལུ་མ་ཅིག་	ཚ་ལུ་མ་གཅིག་
an orange	an orange	one orange
མོ་ཊ་ཞིག་	མོ་ཊ་ཅིག	མོ་ཊ་གཅིག་
a motor car	a car	one car
སེམས་ཅན་ཞིག་	སེམས་ཅན་ཅིག་	སེམས་ཅན་གཅིག་
an animal	an animal	one animal
ཉི་གདུགས་ཞིག	ཉི་གདུགས་ཅིག་	ཉི་གདུགས་གཅིག་
an umbrella	an umbrella	one umbrella
སྨྱུ་གུ་ཞིག་	སྨྱུ་གུ་ཅིག་	སྨྱུ་གུ་གཅིག་
a pen	a pen	one pen

ངེས་པའི་ཚིག་གྲོགས། (THE)

The definite article " The"

There is no exact word in Tibetan for this definate article "The". In general demonstrative pronouns ; འདི་ (this) and དེ་ (that) are used often to express the definate article "The".

Examples:

1. མོ་ཊ་དེ་སྔོན་པོ་རེད།

   The car is blue.

2. བག་ལེབ་འདི་ཆེན་པོ་འདུག

   The(loaf of) bread is large.

3. ཁང་མིག་འདི་ཆུང་ཆུང་འདུག

   The room is small.

How to use the verb ཡོད་ in different ways:

ཡོད་ means to exist, to have & is. This can be illustrated by the following examples :

A) The verb ཡོད་ with first person "I & we" which indicates TO EXIST.

1. ང་ཁྲོམ་ལ་ཡོད།

I - market - in - exist

subject - noun - verb

I am in (the) market.

2. ང་བོད་ལ་ཡོད།

I am in Tibet.

3. ང་ལས་ཁུངས་ལ་ཡོད།

I am in (the) office.

4. ང་ཐབ་ཚང་ནང་ལ་ཡོད།

I am in the kitchen.

5. ང་ཚོ་དཔར་ཁང་ལ་ཡོད།

We are in (the) photo studio / we are in (the) printing press.

B) The verb ཡོད་ with first person "I & we" which indicates "TO HAVE".

Examples:

1. ང་ལ་ཞི་མི་ཡོད།

   To - me - cat - have

   I have (a) cat.

2. ང་ལ་དེབ་མང་པོ་ཡོད།

   I have many books.

3. ང་ལ་ཆུ་ཚོད་ཅིག་ཡོད།

   I have a watch.

4. ང་ཚོ་ལ་དཔར་ཆས་ཡོད།

   We have (a) camera.

5. ང་ཚོ་ལ་མེ་ཏོག་ལྡུམ་ར་ཡོད།

   We have (a) flower garden.

C) When first person possessive ངའི་ (my) ང་ཚོའི་ (our) are used with an object; the verb ཡོད་ indicates " IS ".

Examples:

1. ངའི་ཞི་མི་ནང་ལ་ཡོད།

   My cat is in (the) house.

2. ང་ཚོའི་ཕྲུ་གུ་སློབ་གྲྭར་ཡོད།

Our children are in (the) school.

3. ངའི་དངུལ་དངུལ་ཁང་ལ་ཡོད།

My money is in (the) bank.

4. ང་ཚོའི་དོ་པོ་མོ་ཊའི་ནང་ལ་ཡོད།

Our luggage is in (the) car.

5. ངའི་དེབ་ཅོག་ཙེ་སྟེང་ལ་ཡོད།

My book is on (the) table.

D) When second person possessive ཁྱེད་རང་གི་ (your) is used with an object ; the verb ཡོད་ indicates " IS ".

Examples:

1. ཁྱེད་རང་གི་དཔར་ཆས་སྒམ་གྱི་ནང་ལ་ཡོད།

Your camera is in (the) box.

2. ཁྱེད་རང་ཚོའི་དེབ་ཚེ་རིང་ལ་ཡོད།

Your book is with Tsering.

3. ཁྱེད་རང་གི་སྨྱུ་གུ་ང་ལ་ཡོད།

Your pen is with me.

D) In the same way when third person possessive ཁོང་གི་ (his / her) ཁོང་ཚོའི་ (their) are used with an object; the verb ཡོད་ indicates " IS ".

Examples:

1. ཁོང་གི་ཞྭ་མོ་སྒམ་གྱི་སྟེང་ལ་ཡོད།

   His hat is on (the) box.

2. ཁོང་ཚོའི་མོ་ཊ་ཐང་ལ་ཡོད།

   Their car is on (the) ground.

3. ཁོང་ཚོའི་བུ་མོ་སློབ་གྲྭར་ཡོད།

   Their daughter is in (the) school.

How to use འདུག and ཡོག་རེད་ in the different ways :

1. འདུག is used for first hand visual knowledge
2. ཡོག་རེད་ is used for the less certain, second hand knowledge or commonly known situations.

   འདུག / ཡོག་རེད་ means to exist, have & has in the second and third person:

   Examples:

1. ཁྱེད་རང་ཁྲོམ་ལ་འདུག / ཡོག་རེད།

   You-in(the) -market-existed / You were in the market.

2. ཁྱེད་རང་ལྡི་ལི་ལ་འདུག / ཡོག་རེད།

You were in Delhi.

3. ཁྱེད་རང་གཙུག་ལག་ཁང་ལ་འདུག / ཡོག་རེད།

You were at (the) temple.

4. ཁྱེད་རང་ དངུལ་ཁང་ལ་འདུག /ཡོག་རེད།

You were in (the) bank.

5. ཁྱེད་རང་ཟ་ཁང་ལ་འདུག / ཡོག་རེད།

You were in (the) restaurant.

Note : The above sentences indicate the " past tense".

ཡོག་པ་རེད། and ཡོད་རེད། are used in the literary form.

ཡོག་རེད། is used only in the spoken language.

འདུག / ཡོག་རེད། which means " HAVE "

Examples:

1. ཁྱེད་རང་ལ་ཞི་མི་འདུག / ཡོག་རེད།

You - to - cat - have. (have)

You have (a) cat.

2. ཁྱེད་རང་ལ་དཔར་ཆས་ཤིག་འདུག / ཡོག་རེད།

You have a camera.

3. ཁྱེད་རང་ལ་ཤིང་ཏོག་མང་པོ་འདུག / ཡོག་རེད།

You have a lot of fruit.

4. ཁྱེད་རང་ལ་རླུང་འཕྲིན་འདུག / ཡོག་རེད།

You have (a) radio.

5. ཁྱེད་རང་ལ་སྨྱུ་གུ་འདུག / ཡོག་རེད།

You have (a) pen.

In general, in the first person possessive, the verb ཡོད་ is used to indicate a definate statement. འདུག / ཡོག་རེད་ are also used in the first person possessive. This indicates something that is found to be definate only after investigation. ཡོག་རེད་ also indicates the commonly known situations.

Examples:

1. ངའི་བུ་སློབ་གྲྭར་ཡོད། འདུག / ཡོག་རེད།

My son is in the school.

2. ང་ཚོའི་དཔར་ཆས་སྒམ་གྱི་ནང་ལ་ཡོད། འདུག /ཡོག་རེད།

Our camera is in the box.

3. ངའི་སྨྱུ་གུ་ཁྱེད་རང་ལ་ཡོད། འདུག / ཡོག་རེད།

You have my. pen.

འདུག / ཡོག་རེད། are also used in the second person possessive.

Examples:

1. ཁྱེད་རང་གི་དེབ་སློབ་གྲྭར་འདུག / ཡོག་རེད།

Your book is in the school.

2. ཁྱེད་རང་གི་ཡི་གེ་སྦྲག་ཁང་ལ་འདུག / ཡོག་རེད།

Your letter is in the post office.

3. ཁྱེད་རང་ཚོའི་པ་ལགས་བོད་ལ་འདུག / ཡོག་རེད།

Your (plural) father is in Tibet.

འདུག / ཡོག་རེད། which means " *Exist* " and are used in the third person possessive.

Examples:

1. ཁོང་གི་བུ་ནང་ལ་འདུག / ཡོག་རེད།

His / her son is at home.

2. ཁོང་གི་བུ་མོ་སློབ་གྲྭར་འདུག / ཡོག་རེད།

His / her daughter is in the school.

3. ཁོང་ཚོའི་ཨ་མ་ལགས་ཉི་ཧོང་ལ་འདུག / ཡོག་རེད།

Their mother is in Japan.

In general, the verb ཡོད་ is used when a sentence begins with ང་ལ་ (nga-la) i.e.

ང་ལ་ཡི་གེ་གཉིས་ཡོད།

I have two letters.

The verb འདུག is also used in the first person ང་ལ་ but this indicates something that is found to be definate only after one has been informed by someone. For example : One has found one or more letters in the mail box or has been given them directly by the postman.

Examples:

1. ང་ལ་ཡི་གེ་གཉིས་འདུག

There are two letters for me.

2. ང་ལ་བྱ་ག་རག་འདུག

I got a prize.

The verb ཡོག་རེད། is used in the first person ང་ལ་ but this indicates a high expectation.

Examples:

1. ང་ལ་ཡི་གེ་ཡོག་རེད།

   I must have a letter.

2. ང་ལ་བྱ་དགའ་རག་ཡོག་རེད།

   I am sure to get a prize.

The verb ཡོག་རེད། is also used in the first person ང་ལ་ to indicate something remembered, although the details are unclear.

Examples:

1. ང་ལ་སྒྲུང་དེབ་ཅིག་ཡོག་རེད།

   I (used to) have a story book.

2. ང་ཚོ་ལ་ཡིག་ཆ་འགའ་ཤས་ཡོག་རེད།

   We (used to) have some documents.

Use of རེད

རེད་ which means " Yes " " Is / Are "

རེད་ in general an auxiliary verb " to be "

Notes :

1. When རེད་ (re) is used alone, it means " Yes ".
2. When auxiliary verb རེད་ is used in a sentence in singular, it means " Is ".
3. The auxiliary verb རེད་ is used in a sentence in the plural, it means " Are ".

Examples:

1. དྲི་བ། འདི་མོ་ཊ་རེད་པས། ལན། རེད།

   Question: Is this a car? Ans: Yes.

2. ཁོང་བླ་མ་རེད།

   He is (a) Lama.

3. དེ་མུ་ཟེའི་སྒམ་རེད།

   That is (a) match box.

4. ཁོང་ཟླ་བ་ལགས་རེད།

   He is Dawa la.

5. འདི་མེ་ཏོག་རེད།

This is (a) flower.

When auxiliary verb རེད་ (re) is used in a sentence in the plural, it means " Are ".

Examples:

1. ཁྱེད་རང་ཚོ་གྲྭ་པ་རེད།

You are monks.

2. དེ་ཚོ་དེབ་རེད།

Those are books.

3. ཁོང་ཚོ་མཁས་པ་རེད།

They are scholars.

དྲི་ཚིག་ཁག

Interrogative Particles :

Interrogative particles གམ་ ངམ་ དམ་ ནམ་ བམ་ མམ་ འམ་ རམ་ ལམ་ སམ་ ཏམ་ are used in literary form.

Examples:

1. ཁོང་ཁྲོམ་ལ་འདུག་གམ།

   Is he/she in the market?

2. ཁྱེད་རང་ལ་ཡི་གེ་བྱུང་ངམ།

   Did you get (a) letter?

3. ཁྱེད་རང་ལ་ཁང་པ་ཡོད་དམ།

   Do you have a house?

4. འདི་ཁྱེད་རང་གི་མིན་ནམ།

   Isn't it yours ?

5. འདི་ཁབ་བམ།

   Is it (a) needle?

6. རྙོག་ཁྲ་འཇམ་མམ།

   Has the problem been solved ?

7. དེ་འཇའ་འམ། / དེ་འཇའམ།

   Is that(a) rainbow ?

8. འདི་གྲོང་ཁྱེར་རམ།

Is this (a) town ?

9. འདི་བལ་ལམ།

Is it wool ?

10. ཁོང་ཕེབས་སམ།

Did he/she come ? / Did he/she go ?

11. ཀྲུ་རད་ཏམ། ལྷ་སུ།

In colloquial Tibetan the interrogative particles i.e. གས་ ངས་ པས་ or བས་ are used for the first person ང་ (I) and ང་ཚོ་ (we), the second person ཁྱེད་རང (you) and ཁྱེད་རང་ཚོ་ (you pl.), The third person ཁོང་(he / she) & ཁོང་ཚོ་ (they).

Rules to use three interrogative particles (དྲི་ཚིག་) གས། ངས། & པས or བས། in the spoken language.

The interrogative particle གས། is used after the suffix ག་

The interrogative particle ངས། is used after the suffix ང་

The interrogative particle པས། is used after suffixes

ན་ བ་ མ་ ས་

The interrogative particle བས། is used after suffixes

ད་ འ་ ར་ ལ་

In colloquial Tibetan language these interrogative particles གས་ ངས་ བས་ & པས་ are used in a question which requires the answer either " Yes or No ".

Examples:

1. འདི་ཁྱེད་རང་གི་དཔར་ཆས་རེད་བས།

   Is this your camera ?

2. ཁྱེད་རང་ཁྲོམ་ལ་ཕེབས་ཀྱི་ཡིན་པས།

   Are you going to the market ?

3. ཁོང་བཞེས་ཐག་མཆོད་ཀྱི་ཡོག་རེད་བས།

   Does he/she smoke cigarettes ?

4. ཁྱེད་རང་སྒྲོལ་དཀར་ལགས་ཡིན་པས།

   Are you Dolkar la ?

5. ཁོང་ཁྲོམ་ལ་འདུག་གས།

   Is he/she in the market ?

6. ངའི་དེབ་ཁྱེད་རང་ལ་བྱུང་ངས།

   Did you get my book ?

Interrogative adverbs and pronouns :

ག་གི་	which	ག་དུས་	when	ག་པར་	where
སུ་	who	སུ་ལ་	whom	ག་རེ་	what
ག་རེ་བྱས་ནས་	why	ག་འདྲས་ཟེ་(ཟེར་)	how	སུའི་	whose

The above mentioned interrogative adverbs and pronouns are appeared in the sentences, the interrogative particles

གས། ངས། བས། & པས། are not used.

Examples:

1. ཁྱེད་རང་དེབ་ག་གི་ཀློག་གནང་གི་ཡིན།

   Which book do you want to read ?

2. ཁྱེད་རང་ཁྲོམ་ལ་ག་དུས་ཕེབས་གནང་གི་ཡིན།

   When are you going to the market ?

3. ཁྱེད་རང་ག་པར་ཕྱག་ལས་གནང་གི་ཡོད།

   Where are you working ?

4. ཁོང་ ག་རེ་གནང་གི་འདུག

   What is he doing ?

5. བག་ལེབ་འདི་ག་འདྲས་ཟེ་བཟོ་དགོས་རེད།

   How do (you) make this bread ?

Rules to use tense verb endings or verb complements in the interrogative form or particles.

In interrogative particles the verb complements of the first person i.e

གི་ཡིན། *(future tense)* གི་ཡོད། *(present tense)*

པ་ཡིན། *(past tense)* are used in the second person

ཁྱེད་རང་། ཁྱེད་རང་ཚོ་ *(you singular & you plural)* when

a sentence indicate the question.

Examples:

1. ཁྱེད་རང་དྲི་ལི་ལ་ཕེབས་ཀྱི་ཡིན་པས།

   Are you going to Delhi ?

2. ཁྱེད་རང་ཚོ་ཟ་ཁང་ལ་ཕེབས་པས།

   Did you go to the restaurant ?

3. ཁྱེད་རང་འཆམ་འཆམ་ལ་ཐེག་གི་ཡོད་པས།

   Are you going for a walk ?

4. ཁྱེད་རང་གསོལ་ཇ་མངར་མོ་མཆོད་ཀྱི་ཡིན་པས།

   Are you going to drink sweet tea ?

The verb complements of the second person i.e.

གི་རེད། *(future tense)*

གི་འདུག། *(present tense)*

པ་རེད། བ་རེད། སོང་། *(past tense)* These verb

complements are used in the first person interrogative

participle.

Examples:

1. ང་ལྡི་ལི་ལ་འགྲོ་གི་རེད་པས།

   Will I go to Delhi ?

2. ང་འཆམ་འཆམ་ལ་འགྲོ་གི་འདུག་གས།

   Am I going for a walk ?

The verb complements of the third person will remain the same in the interrogative participle.

Examples:

1. ཁོང་ལྡི་ལི་ལ་ཕེབས་ཀྱི་རེད་པས།

   Will she go to Delhi ?

2. ཁོང་གསོལ་ཇ་མངར་མོ་མཆོད་ཀྱི་འདུག་གས།

   Is she drinking tea ?

3. ཁོང་འཆམ་འཆམ་ལ་ཕེབས་སོང་ངས།

   Did she go for a walk ?

Use of བྱུང་/ སོང་ and ཤག་

A) བྱུང་ is a main verb which means "got" and is used for the first person only.

Examples:

1. ང་ལ་ཡི་གེ་ཞིག་བྱུང་།

   To me-letter-a-got.

   I got a letter.

2. ང་ལ་དེབ་ཅིག་བྱུང་།

   I got a book.

The same བྱུང (jung) is also used as an auxiliary verb of the past tense and is used only for the first person.

Examples:

1. ཁྱེད་རང་གིས་ང་ལ་བོད་ཡིག་བསླབས་བྱུང་།

   You taught me Tibetan.

2. ཁོང་གིས་ང་ལ་མོ་ཊ་ཞིག་གནང་བྱུང་།

   He/she gave me a car.

3. ཁོང་གིས་ང་ལ་ཡི་གེ་བཏང་བྱུང་།

   He/she sent me (a) letter.

The main verb བྱུང་ (*jung*) and the auxiliary verb བྱུང་ are converted into negative by adding མ་ (*ma*) right before the བྱུང་། Thus : བྱུང་ (positive) མ་བྱུང་ (negative)

Examples:

1. ང་ལ་དེབ་མ་བྱུང་།

   I didn't get (a) book.

2. ཁྱེད་རང་གིས་ང་ལ་བོད་ཡིག་བསླབས་མ་བྱུང་།

   You didn't teach me Tibetan.

3. ཁོང་གིས་ཁྱེད་རང་ལ་བཀའ་འདྲི་གནང་མ་སོང་།

   He didn't ask you (a) question.

B) སོང་། [*song*]

སོང་། (*song*) is an auxiliary verb of the past tense and is used for the second and third person. We use this type of auxiliary verb when the reporter has seen the person finishing a work which he was doing. It is notnecessary that he or she should see the work right from the beginning.

Examples: [second person]

1. ཁྱེད་རང་གིས་ཁོང་ལ་བོད་ཡིག་བསླབས་སོང་།

   You taught him Tibetan.

2. ཁྱེད་རང་གིས་ཁོང་ལ་བཀའ་འདྲི་ཞུས་སོང་།

You asked her a question.

3. ཁྱེད་རང་གིས་ཁོང་ལ་ཡི་གེ་བཏང་སོང་།

You sent him a letter.

Examples : [Third person]

1. ཁོང་གིས་ཁྱེད་རང་ལ་བོད་ཡིག་བསླབས་སོང་།

He/ she taught you Tibetan.

2. ཁོང་གིས་ཁྱེད་རང་ལ་ཕྱུག་དངུལ་གནང་སོང་།

He gave (some) money to you.

3. ཁོང་གིས་ཁྱེད་རང་ལ་ཕྱུག་དེབ་ཅིག་གནང་སོང་།

She gave you a book.

The auxiliary verb སོང་ (song) can be changed into nagative by adding a མ་ (ma) right before སོང་།

Thus: སོང་ (positive) མ་སོང་ (negative)

Examples :

1. ཁྱེད་རང་གིས་ཁོང་ལ་བོད་ཡིག་བསླབས་མ་སོང་།

You did not teach him/her Tibetan.

2. ཁོང་གིས་ཁྱེད་རང་ལ་ཕྱུག་དངུལ་གནང་མ་སོང་།

She didn't give you money.

C) ཤག [shag]

When ཤག (shag) is used for the first person. It shows that the action was done without intention or without one being conscious of what one was doing.

Examples :

1. ངས་ཐད་དེ་བརྗེད་ཤག

   I forgot completely.

2. ང་གཉིད་འཁུགས་ཤག

   I fell asleep.

3. ངའི་དཔར་ཆས་བརླགས་ཤག

   I lost my camera.

To change the above sentences into negative; ཤག་ (shag) is converted into མེད།

Examples :

1. ངས་ཐད་དེ་བརྗེད་མེད།

   I didn't forget completely.

2. ང་གཉིད་འཁུགས་མེད།

   I didn't sleep.

3. ངའི་དཔར་ཆས་བརླགས་མེད།

   I didn't loose my camera.

ཤག (shag) is also used as an auxiliary verb of the past tense and is used for second and third person. In this case the reporter has not seen the person doing the work but has second hand knowledge through some one or from the news papers etc.

Examples : [Second person]

1. ཁྱེད་རང་གིས་ཁོང་ལ་བོད་ཡིག་བསླབས་ཤག

   You taught him Tibetan.

2 ཁྱེད་རང་གིས་ཁོང་ལ་བཀའ་འདྲི་གནང་ཤག

   You asked him (a) question.

3. ཁྱེད་རང་གིས་ཁོང་ལ་གསུངས་ཤག

   You told him /her.

Examples : [Third person]

1. ཁོང་གིས་ཁྱེད་རང་ལ་བོད་ཡིག་བསླབས་ཤག

   He taught you Tibetan language.

2. ཁོང་གིས་ཁྱེད་རང་ལ་བཀའ་ལན་གནང་ཤག

   He answered your questions.

Some of the negative sentences :

1. ཁྱེད་རང་གིས་ཁོང་ལ་བོད་ཡིག་བསླབས་མི་འདུག

   You didn't teach him/her Tibetan.

2. ཁོང་གིས་ཁྱེད་རང་ལ་བཀའ་འདྲི་གནང་མི་འདུག

He/she didn't ask you a question.

འབྲེལ་སྒྲ། Genetives & Possessives

གི་ ཀྱི་ གྱི་ ཡི་ & འི་ are five genetives.

Grammatical rules to use the genetives in literary forms :

གི་ is used after suffix ག་ & ང་

ཀྱི་ is used after suffixes ད་ བ་ & ས་

གྱི་ is used after suffixes ན་ མ་ ར་ & ལ་

ཡི་ & འི་ are used after suffix འ་ & མཐའ་མེད།

(མཐའ་མེད་: An independent root letter without suffix)

The above mentioned grammatical rules are summarized on a chart with examples. [see page No. 180]

In general, in ordinary colloquial Tibetan, the above mentioned grammatical rules of sentence construction for genitives and possessives are not followed strictly,especially when such construction would impede the ease of movement of the tongue. Therefore, in ordinary spoken language genitive གི་ is used often instead of ཀྱི་ གྱི་ & ཡི་

Examples :

1. ང་འགྲོ་གི་ཡོད། (ཡི་)

   I am going.

2. ང་ལས་ཀ་བྱེད་གི་ཡོད། (ཀྱི་)

   I will work.

3. མོ་དེབ་ལེན་གི་འདུག (གྱི་)

   She is taking (some) books.

བྱེད་སྒྲ། Instrumentals

གིས་ is used after suffix ག་ & ང་

ཀྱིས་ is used after suffixes ད་ བ་ & ས་

གྱིས་ is used after suffixes ན་ མ་ ར་ & ལ་

ཡིས་ is used after suffix འ་ & མཐའ་མེད།

The instrumental or agent is expressed by the particles གིས་ ཀྱིས་ གྱིས་ & ཡིས་

Examples :

1. ཁོང་གིས་གསོལ་ཇ་མཆོད་སོང་།

   He/she drank tea.

2. ཐང་ཀ་འདི་ཟླ་བ་ལགས་ཀྱིས་བྲིས་པ་རེད།

This Thangka is painted by Dawa.

3. རྒྱན་ཆ་འདི་དངུལ་གྱིས་བཟོས་པ་རེད།

This ornament is made of silver.

4. ང་ཡིས་བག་ལེབ་བཟོས་པ་ཡིན།/ ངས་བག་ལེབ་བཟོས་པ་ཡིན།

I made (this) bread.

Instrumental or agent is also used with an independent root letter simply by adding ས་ (sa).

Examples :

1. ང + ས་ = ངས་ by me

ངས་དེབ་འདི་ཀློག་ས་པ་ཡིན།

I read this book.

2. ཁོ + ས་ = ཁོས་ by him/her

ཡི་གེ་འདི་ཁོས་བྲིས་པ་རེད།

He wrote this letter.

3. ང་ཚོ + ས་ = ང་ཚོས་ by us

ང་ཚོས་ཁྲོམ་ནས་ཚལ་ཉོས་པ་ཡིན།

We bought vegetables from the market.

4. དེ + ས་ = དེས་ by that

མི་དེས་ཆང་མང་པོ་བཏུངས་སོང་།

That man drank a lot of chang*.

Note In ordinary colloquial Tibetan conversation instrumental ཀྱིས་/ གྱིས་ are not followed strictly according to the grammatical rules. But is often used to allow easier speach flow. Therefore, ཀྱིས/གྱིས་ are often replaced by གི་ in colloquial language.

---

* Tibetan beer

དགག་སྒྲ་བཞི།

Four negative particles

མ་ མི་ མིན་ & མེད་ are called four negative particles.

མ་ & མི་ are used directly before the verb

Examples :

མ་བྱེད་ " don't do "

མི་དགོས་ " don't want "

མིན་ & མེད་ are the verbs in the negative and always appear at the end of the sentence.

Examples :

ང་ཚེ་རིང་མིན།	I am not Tsering.
ང་ལ་ལས་ཀ་བྱེད་ལོང་མེད།	I don't have time to work.

Positive form		Negative form
རེད་	is changed into	མ་རེད།
བྱུང་	is changed into	མ་བྱུང་
སོང་	is changed into	མ་སོང་
འདུག	is changed into	མི་འདུག

Examples :

	Positive	Negative
1.	ཁོང་ཟླ་བ་རེད།	ཁོང་ཟླ་བ་མ་རེད།
	He is Dawa.	He is not Dawa.
2.	ང་ལ་ཡི་གེ་འབྱོར་བྱུང་།	ང་ལ་ཡི་གེ་འབྱོར་མ་བྱུང་།
	I received (a) letter.	I didn't receive (a) letter.
3.	ཁོང་ཁྲོམ་ལ་འདུག	ཁོང་ཁྲོམ་ལ་མི་འདུག
	She is in the market.	She is not in the market.
4.	ང་བཀྲ་ཤིས་ཡིན།	ང་བཀྲ་ཤིས་མིན་།
	I am Tashi.	I am not Tashi.
5.	ང་ལ་དཔར་ཆས་ གཉིས་ཡོད།	ང་ལ་དཔར་ཆས་གཉིས་མེད།
	I have two cameras.	I don't have two cameras.

Note : 1. In colloquial Tibetan language མི་འདུག (mi–dug) is pronounced as min-dug.

2. མིན་(min) is also pronounced as མན་(man) in spoken language.

The negative particle མ་ (ma) is sometimes used inbetween two nouns. This indicates that the two primary components of meaning are separated by the negative particle མ་ (ma) .

Examples :

གངས་མ་ཆར་	" not-snow-not rain ," i.e. " slush; "
ར་མ་ལུག་	" not-goat - not-sheep," i.e. "mixture".
བྱ་མ་རྟ་	"not-bird not-horse," i.e. "messenger."

Use of རང་ (rang) in different ways with different meanings

1. རང་ which means "self". This is used with pronouns.

Examples :

1. ཁྱེད་རང་བོད་ལ་ཕེབས་ཀྱི་ཡིན་པས།

   Are you going to Tibet ?

2. ཁོང་རང་དིལླི་ལ་ཕེབས་ཀྱི་རེད།

   He/she will go to Delhi.

3. ཕྱག་དེབ་འདི་ཁྱེད་རང་གི་རེད།

   This is your book.

4. ཁོང་རང་ཁ་སང་ཨ་རི་ལ་ཕེབས་སོང་།

   He/she went to America yesterday.

5. ང་རང་བོད་ལ་ཕྱིན་པ་ཡིན།

   I went to Tibet.

2. རང་ is also used as an emphasizing pronouns.

such as : ང་རང་རང་ (myself) ཁྱེད་རང་རང་ (yourself)

ཁོང་རང་རང་ (him/herself) ང་ཚོ་རང (ourselves)

ཁོང་ཚོ་རང་ (themselves) དེ་རང་རང་ (itself)

Examples : [see page number 32.]

3. རང་ which means "so / too". This is always used with an adjective in the negative and positive sentences. In general རང་ (rang) is often used in the negative sense.

Examples :

1. སྨྱུ་གུ་འདི་ཡག་པོ་རང་མི་འདུག

This pen is not so good.

2 བོད་ཀྱི་སྐད་ཡིག་ཁག་པོ་རང་མི་འདུག

The Tibetan language is not so difficult.

3. ཀུ་ཤུ་འདི་ཞིམ་པོ་རང་མི་འདུག

This apple is not so delicious.

4. ཁང་པ་འདི་ཆེན་པོ་རང་མི་འདུག

This room is not so big.

5. མི་འདི་ཡག་པོ་རང་མི་འདུག

This man is not so good.

6. དེ་རིང་གྲང་མོ་རང་མི་འདུག

Today, it's not too cold.

4. རང་ which means "just". This is used after ད་ལྟ་ (now) , དེ་རིང་ (today), སང་ཉིན་ (tomorrow), ཁ་སྔ་ (yesterday), ཁ་སྔ་ཞོགས་ཀད་ (yesterday morning), འདི་ལོ་ (this year), ན་ནིང་ (last year) etc. which indicates the time.

Examples :

1. ངས་ཁོང་ད་ལྟ་རང་མཇལ་བྱུང་།

I met him/her just now.

2. ཁོང་ཁ་སྔ་རང་དངུལ་ཁང་ལ་ཕེབས་སོང་།

He/she went to the bank just yesterday.

3. ང་ཚོས་མོ་ཊ་འདི་ན་ནིང་རང་ཉོས་པ་ཡིན།

We bought this car just last year.

4. ངས་ཁ་སྔ་ཞོགས་ཀད་རང་ཡི་གེ་ཞིག་བཏང་པ་ཡིན།

I sent a letter just yesterday morning.

4. ཁྱེད་རང་གདང་དགོང་རང་ཁྲོམ་ལ་མཇལ་བྱུང་།

I met you just yesterday in the market.

5. རང་ is also used with places which means " itself "

Examples :

1. ཁོང་ལྷ་ས་རང་ནས་རེད།

He /she is from Lhasa (itself).

2 ངའི་དབྱར་ཁའི་གུང་སེང་ལྡི་ལི་རང་ལ་བཏང་པ་ཡིན།

I spent my summer holiday in Delhi (itself) .

3. ང་ཨུ་རུ་སུ་རང་ལ་ཕྱིན་པ་ཡིན།

I went to Russia (itself).

verbal compounds which consist of a noun / verb. This is a particular Tibetan construction.

A) ས་ (sa) place / space

In literary and colloquial Tibetan when ས་ (sa) is added right after a verb, the meaning of the verb will be changed.

Thus :

1. འཐུང་ས་ place to drink / container to drink
2. ཀློག་ས་ place to read
3. ཉོ་ས་ place to buy
4. ཚོང་ས་ place to sell
5. བཟོ་ས་ place to make

Examples :

1. འདི་ཇ་འཐུང་ས་རེད།

This is a place to drink tea. OR This is a container for drinking tea.

2. ཕ་གི་དེབ་ཀློག་ས་རེད།

That is the place for reading books.

3. འདི་ཚལ་ཉོ་ས་རེད།

This is the place for buying vegetables.

4. དེ་དཀར་ཡོལ་བཟོ་ས་རེད།

That is the place which makes cups.

5. དེ་གནམ་གྲུའི་ཀྲི་ཀ་སི་ཚོང་ས་རེད།

That is a place which sells air tickets.

B) ལོང་ (long) " time " (time to do something)

The meaning will also changed when this ལོང (long)

is added right after a verb,

Thus :

1. འཐུང་ལོང་ time to drink
2. ཀློག་ལོང་ time to read
3. ཉོ་ལོང time to buy
4. ཚོང་ལོང་ time to sell
5. བཟོ་ལོང་ time to make

Examples :

1. ང་ལ་ཇ་འཐུང་ལོང་མེད།

I don't have time to drink tea.

2. ཡི་གེ་འདི་ཀློག་ལོང་ཡོད་པས།

Do (you) have time to read this letter?

3. ཁྱེད་རང་ལ་ཚལ་གཟིགས་ལོང་ཡོད་པས།

Do you have time to buy vegetables.

4. ང་ལ་ཞལ་ལག་བཟོ་ལོང་མེད།

I don't have time to make food.

5. ཁོང་ལ་ཀུ་ཤུ་ཚོང་ལོང་ཡོག་རེད།

He/she has time to sell apples.

C) དུས་ when / while

1. འགྲོ་དུས་ when / while going
2. ཉོ་དུས་ when / while purchasing
3. ཚོང་དུས་ when / while selling
4. བཟོ་དུས་ when / while making
5. ཉལ་དུས་ when / while sleeping

Examples :

1. ང་བལ་ཡུལ་ལ་ཡོད་དུས་ཁོང་མཇལ་བྱུང་།

I met him while I was in Nepal.

2. ང་དཔར་ཆས་ཉོ་དུས་ཡག་ཉེས་སྐད་ཆ་དྲིས་པ་ཡིན།

I asked about the quality while I was purchasing a camera.

3. ཁོང་ཆང་ཚོང་དུས་ངས་ཀུ་ཤུ་གཉིས་ཉོས་པ་ཡིན།

I bought two apples while she was selling chang. *

4. ཁྱེད་རང་གཟིམ་དུས་ངས་ཇ་བཟོས་པ་ཡིན།

I prepared tea while you were sleeping.

5. ཁྱེད་རང་བག་ལེབ་བཟོ་དུས་ངས་ཚལ་བཟོས་པ་ཡིན།

I made (some) vegetables while you were making bread.

D) སྐབས་ " when / while " This is used often in literary Tibetan but it's also used in the colloquial Tibetan.

Thus :

1. འབྲི་སྐབས་ when / while writing
2. ཤོད་སྐབས་ when / while telling
3. ཡོད་སྐབས་ when / while exist
4. བྱེད་སྐབས་ when / while doing

---

* ཆང་ Tibetan beer

Examples :

1. ང་ཡི་གེ་འབྲི་སྐབས་ཁོང་ལྡི་ལི་ནས་ཕེབས་བྱུང་།

He/she arrived from Delhi when I was writing a letter.

2 ང་ཚོ་སྐད་ཆ་ཤོད་སྐབས་ཁྱེད་རང་ཕེབས་མ་བྱུང་།

You didn't come when we were discussing (a matter).

3. ང་ཚོ་བོད་ལ་ཡོད་པའི་སྐབས་ཁྱེད་རང་མཇལ་བྱུང་།

We met you when you were in Tibet.

4. ཁྱེད་རང་དྷ་རམ་ས་ལར་སློབ་སྦྱོང་གནང་སྐབས་ཟླ་བ་ལགས་མཇལ་བྱུང་ངས།

Did you see Dawa la when you were studying in Dharamsala?

E) འདོད་ "want / wish" This expresses one's desire.

1.	འཐུང་འདོད་	want to drink
2.	ཀློག་འདོད་	want to read
3.	སློབ་སྦྱོང་བྱེད་འདོད་	want to study
4.	འབྲི་འདོད་	want to write
5.	བཟོ་འདོད་	want to make

Examples :

1. ང་ཚ་ལུ་མའི་ཁུ་བ་འཐུང་འདོད་ཡོད། [འདུག]

   I want to drink (some) orange juice.

2 ང་ཚོ་སྒྲུང་དེབ་ཀློག་འདོད་ཡོད།

   We want to read (some) story books.

3. ཁྱེད་རང་དཔེ་མཛོད་ཁང་ལ་སློབ་སྦྱོང་བྱེད་འདོད་ཡོད་པས།

   Do you want to study at the Library?

4. ཁྱེད་རང་དེབ་ཅིག་འབྲི་འདོད་ཡོད་པས།

   Do you want to write a book?

5. དེ་རིང་ང་ཐུག་པ་བཟོ་འདོད་ཡོད།

   Today, I want to make (some) noodles.

F) སྙིང་འདོད་ " want / wish " This expresses a stronger desire.

Thus :

1. འཐུང་སྙིང་འདོད་ really want to drink
2. ཀློག་སྙིང་འདོད་ really want to read
3. བཟོ་སྙིང་འདོད་ really want to make
4. འགྲོ་སྙིང་འདོད་ really want to go

Examples :

1. དེ་རིང་ང་བོད་ཇ་འཐུང་སྙིང་འདོད་ཀྱི་འདུག

Today, I really want to drink Tibetan tea.

2 ང་དེབ་ཀློག་སྙིང་འདོད་ཀྱི་འདུག

I really want to read a book.

3. ང་ཚལ་མོག་མོག་བཟོ་སྙིང་འདོད་ཀྱི་འདུག

I really want to make (some) vegetable momos.

4. ང་བོད་ལ་འགྲོ་སྙིང་འདོད་ཀྱི་འདུག

I really want to go to Tibet.

G) རྩིས་ "planning to" (do something)

1. བྱེད་རྩིས་ plan to do
2. མངག་རྩིས་ plan to order
3. སློབ་སྦྱོང་བྱེད་རྩིས་ plan to study
4. ཡོང་རྩིས་ plan to come
5. བསྒྱུར་རྩིས་ plan to translate

Examples :

1. དེ་རིང་ང་སློབ་སྦྱོང་བྱེད་རྩིས་ཡོད།

Today, I am planning to study.

2 ང་བཞིས་ཚལ་དང་ བཞིས་འབྲས་མངག་རྩིས་ཡོད།

I am planning to order vegetable and rice.

3. ང་ད་དུང་མཐོ་སློབ་ནང་ལ་ལོ་གཉིས་སློབ་སྦྱོང་བྱེད་རྩིས་ཡོད།

I am still planning to study at the university for two years.

4. ང་ལོ་རྗེས་མ་ཡོང་རྩིས་ཡོད།

I am planning to come next year.

5. ང་དེབ་འགའ་ཤས་བོད་ཡིག་ནང་བསྒྱུར་རྩིས་ཡོད།

I am planning to translate some books in Tibetan language.

F རན་ " time to " (do something)

1. ཐོན་རན་ time to leave / go
2. བཟོ་རན་ time to make
3. མཆོད་རན་ time to eat / drink
4. འགྲོ་རན་ time to go
5. མངག་རན་ time to order

Examples :

1. ང་ཚོ་སློབ་གྲྭར་འགྲོ་རན་འདུག

   It is time for us to go to the school.

2 ཉིན་གུང་གསོལ་ཚིགས་བཟོ་རན་འདུག

   It is time to make lunch.

3. དགོང་དྲོའི་གསོལ་ཚིགས་མཆོད་རན་འདུག་གས།

   Is it time to eat dinner?

4. ང་ཚོ་བོད་ལ་ཐོན་རན་འདུག

   It is time for us to go to Tibet.

5. ཉི་ཧོང་ནས་དཔར་ཆས་འགའ་ཤས་མངག་རན་འདུག

   It is time to order some cameras from Japan.

Use of མཁན་

མཁན་ " Doer or agent " "the goer"

Such as : བཟོ་མཁན་ (maker), ཚོང་མཁན་ (seller),

གཅོད་མཁན་(cutter), ཀློག་མཁན་(reader) and

འགྲོ་མཁན་ (goer).

མཁན་ is extensively used in the colloquial to signify a person who, in some capacity or character, is connected with some particular act, state or thing

Examples :

1. ཁོང་བག་ལེབ་བཟོ་མཁན་་རེད།

   He/she is a baker.

2 ཁོང་ཚོ་ཤིང་གཅོད་མཁན་་རེད།

   They are wood cutters.

3. ཁོང་དེབ་ཚོང་མཁན་་རེད།

   He/she is the book seller.

4. ཁོང་གློག་བརྙན་་བཟོ་མཁན་་རེད།

   He is a movie producer.

5. ཁོང་བོད་ལ་འགྲོ་མཁན་་རེད།

   He is the person who will go to Tibet.

Changing of sounds with effect of prefixes to the root letters :

When any one of the three prefixes i.e. ག་ ད་ &. མ་ are used before the root letters ང་ ཉ་ ན་ བ་ མ་ & ཡ་ the sounds of the words will change.

Thus :

1. གཡ*་ ȳa
2. དབ*་ w̄a
3. གན*་ n̄a
4. མན*་ n̄a
5. མཉ*་ n̄ya
6. གཉ*་ n̄ya
7. དམ*་ m̄a
8. མང*་ n̄ga
9. དང*་ n̄ga

Important note : The above mentioned words are best pronounsed with the help of a native Tibetan or some one who knows good Tibetan .

A) གཡ*་ ȳa

Some vocabulary :

1.	གཡག་	yak
2.	གཡས་	right (direction)
3.	གཡོན་	left (direction)
4.	གཡར་	loan, borrow, rent and lend
5.	གཡུ་	turquoise stone
6.	གཡུང་དྲུང་	swastika
7.	གཡོག་པོ་	servant (male)
8.	གཡོག་མོ་	maid / female servant
9.	གཡོགས་	to put on clothes or ornaments on someone or to cover up an object.

Examples :

1. ཕ་གི་གཡག་རེད།

That is a yak.

2 འདི་ངའི་ལག་པ་གཡས་པ་ཡིན།

This is my right hand.

3. ངས་ཁོང་ལ་ཁང་མིག་གཉིས་གཡར་བ་ཡིན།

I have rented two rooms to him.

4. གཡུ་འདི་མདོག་སྔོན་པོ་རེད།

The colour of this turquoise stone is blue.

5. རི་དེའི་གཡོན་ངོས་ལ་ཁང་པ་ཆུང་ཆུང་ཞིག་འདུག

There is a small house on the left side of that mountain.

B) དབ*་ w̄a

Vocabulary :

1. དབང initiation / power
2. དབར inbetween
3. དབེན་པ་ remote place
4. དབུ་ཞྭ་ hat (h)
5. དབུལ་པོ་ poor
6. དབྱེ་བ་ difference
7. དབྱར་ཁ་ summer
8. དབུས་ centre
9. དབྱུག་ throw

Examples :

1. ཁོང་སང་ཉིན་དབང་ཞུ་བར་བཅར་གྱི་རེད།

He will go tomorrow to receive initiation.

2. ཁྱེད་རང་གི་དབུ་ཞྭ་ཆེན་པོ་ཞིད་པོ་ཅིག་འདུག

Your hat is very big.

3. ང་དབྱར་ཁ་བོད་ལ་འགྲོ་གི་ཡིན།

I will go to Tibet in summer.

4. མིང་གཞིའི་ཡི་གེ་བ་དང་ཝ་གཉིས་ལ་དབྱེ་བ་ག་རེ་ཡོད་རེད།

What is the difference between consonant ba and wa?

B) གན*་ w̄a

Vocabulary :

1. གནམ་ sky
2. གནང་ give / do
3. གནངས་ the day after tomorrow
4. གནས་ holy place/ reside
5. གནོད་ harm
6. གནན་ suppress

Examples :

1. གནམ་ལ་གནམ་གྲུ་འགྲོ་གི་འདུག

   An aeroplane is flying in the sky.

2. དེབ་འདི་ཁོང་ལ་གནང་རོགས།

   Please give this book to him.

3. གནངས་ཉིན་ང་ཚོ་བོད་ལ་འགྲོ་གི་ཡིན།

   We will go to Tibet the day after tomorrow.

4. ཀླུ་དེ་རྩ་མིག་དེ་ལ་གནས་ཡོད་པ་རེད།

   The Naga resides in that pond.

5. ཀླུ་དེས་མི་ལ་ག་དུས་ཡིན་ནའང་གནོད་སྐྱེལ་གྱི་མ་རེད།

   That Naga will never harm people.

D) མན་* ṉa

Vocabulary :

1.	མནའ་མ་	bride
2.	མནན་	to press an object
3.	མནག་པོ་	bad (a bad action)
4.	མནལ་ལམ་ (རྨི་ལམ་)	dream
5.	མནའ་	oath

Examples :

1. མནའ་མ་དེ་མོ་ཊའི་ནང་ལ་འདུག

The bride is in the car.

2. ཁྱི་འདི་མོ་ཊའི་འོག་ལ་མནན་པ་རེད།

This dog went under the car.

3. ཁོ་མནག་པོ་ཞེ་དྲག་འདུག

He is very bad. [bad in action]

4. ཁ་སང་ཁྱེད་རང་ལ་མནལ་ལམ་བཟང་པོ་བྱུང་ཤག

Yesterday, you had a good dream.

5. ཁྱེད་རང་ལ་མནའ་སྐྱེལ་དགོས་རེད་གསུངས་བྱུང་ངས།

Are you asked to take an oath ?

E) མཉ*་ n̄a

Vocabulary :

1. མཉམ་དུ་ together / along with
2. མཉེན་པོ་ soft
3. མཉམ་བཞག་ meditation equipose
4. འདྲ་མཉམ་ equal / same
5. སྐུ་མཉེས་ difficult (h)
6. མཉེས་པོ་ good / interesting / like

Examples :

1. ང་ཚོ་ཁྲོམ་ལ་མཉམ་དུ་ཕྱིན་པ་ཡིན།

   We went to the market together. Or

   We went together to the market.

2. ཀོ་བ་འདི་མཉེན་པོ་ཞེ་དྲག་འདུག

   This leather is very soft.

3. ཁོང་ཚོ་ལ་དབང་ཆ་འདྲ་མཉམ་ཡོག་རེད།

   They have the same power.

4. ཞལ་ལག་མཉེས་པོ་འདུག་གས།

   Is the food good ?

5. གཟིགས་མོ་མཉེས་པོ་འདུག

   The show is good / interesting.

F) གཉ*་ n̄ga

Vocabulary :

1. གཉིས་ two
2. གཉེར་པ་ storekeeper
3. གཉེར་ཚང་ store
4. གཉེན་ཚན་ relatives

5. དགེ་བའི་བཤེས་གཉེན་ the root guru / spiritual guru or guide

6. རྒྱབ་གཉེར་ recommendation

7. གཉེར་མ་ wrinkle

8. གཉོམ་ཆུང་ humble

Examples :

1. ང་ལ་གྲོགས་པོ་གཉིས་ཡོད།

I have two friends.

2. ཁོང་གཉེར་པ་རེད།

He is a storekeeper.

3. ཁོང་ང་ཚོའི་གཉེན་ཚན་རེད།

He/she is our relative.

4. རྨོ་འོ་ལགས་དེ་ལ་གཉེར་མ་མང་པོ་འདུག

The grandmother has many wrinkles.

5. བུ་འདི་གཉོམ་ཆུང་ཞེ་དྲག་ཡོག་རེད།

This boy is very humble.

G) དམ*་ m̄a

Vocabulary :

1. དམར་པོ་ red
2. དམག war
3. དམག་མི་ soldier / army
4. མི་དམངས་ people
5. དམུག་ (སྨུག་) bite
6. དམྱལ་བ་ hell
7. དམའ་པོ་ low

Examples :

1. ང་ཚོན་མདོག་དམར་པོ་ལ་དགའ་པོ་མེད།

   I dislike red colours.

2. ང་དམག་ལ་དགའ་པོ་མེད།

   I dislike war.

3. ས་མཚམས་ལ་དམག་མི་མང་པོ་མི་འདུག

   There are not many soldiers on the border.

4. འདི་དམྱལ་བ་གྲང་དམྱལ་ནང་བཞིན་གྲང་མོ་འདུག

   It is as cold as hell.

5. ཁོང་ལ་ཁ་ས་ཁྱིས་དམུག་པ་རེད།

   Yesterday, he was bitten by a dog.

H) མང*་ n̄ga

Vocabulary :

1. མངར་མོ་ sweet
2. མངའ་འོག་ under (under the power)
3. མངལ་ womb
4. མངག་ order
5. མངོན་ feel or appear (literary)

Examples :

1. ཁོང་བཞེས་བག་མངར་མོ་ལ་མཉེས་པོ་ཡོག་རེད།

   He/she likes sweet bread.

2. རྒྱ་གར་དབྱིན་ཇིའི་མངའ་འོག་ལ་ལོ་ཉི་བརྒྱ་བསྡད་པ་རེད།

   India was under the British for two hundred years.

3. ཁོང་གིས་བཞེས་འབྲས་དང་ བཞེས་ཚལ་མངགས་སོང་།

   He ordered (some) rice and vegetables.

I) དང*་ n̄ga

Vocabulary :

1. དངུལ་ silver / money
2. དངོས་པོ་ hings / commodity

3.	དངོས་གནས	real / really
4.	བོད་དངུལ་	Tibetan currency
5.	རྒྱ་གར་གྱི་དངུལ་	Indian rupees
6.	དབྱིན་ཇིའི་དངུལ་	British pounds

Examples :

1. ང་ལ་དངུལ་མང་པོ་མེད།

   I don't have enough money   Or

   I don't have enough silver.

2. ང་བོད་ལ་དངོས་གནས་འགྲོ་གི་ཡིན།

   I will really go to Tibet.

3. དེ་དངོས་གནས་གསེར་རེད།

   That 's real gold.

4. ང་ལ་དབྱིན་ཇིའི་སྒོར་མོ་བརྒྱ་ཐམ་པ་ཡོད།

   I have one hundred British pounds.

How to convert a noun into a verb with the use of the following verbalizers :

གཏོང་ རྒྱག་ & བྱེད་

Present	*Future*	*past*	*meanings*
གཏོང་	གཏང་	བཏང་	to send
རྒྱག་	བརྒྱབ་	བརྒྱབ་	to express an action
བྱེད་	བྱ་/ བྱེད	བྱས་	to do

གཏོང་ *(non-honorific)* གཏོང་གནང་ *(honorific)*

Examples :

A) གཏོང་ (*present tense*)

1. མོ་ཊ་གཏོང་བ་ to drive a car

ང་མོ་ཊ་གཏོང་གི་ཡོད།

I am driving a car.

2. གཞས་གཏོང་བ་ to sing a song

ཁོང་གཞས་གཏོང་གནང་གི་འདུག

He/she is singing a song.

3. ཡི་གེ་གཏོང་བ་ to send a letter / mail

ཁོང་ཡི་གེ་གཏོང་གནང་གི་འདུག

She is sending a letter.

གཏང་ ***(non-honorific)*** གཏང་གནང་ ***(honorific)***

གཏང་ *(future tense)*

1. ཁོང་གིས་ཁྱེད་རང་ལ་ཞལ་དཔར་གཏང་གནང་གི་རེད།

She/he will telephone you.

2. ཁོང་གིས་ཁྱེད་རང་ལ་ཇན་པ་གཏང་གནང་གི་རེད།

She will send you a present.

3. སང་ཉིན་ཆར་པ་གཏང་གི་རེད།

It will rain tomorrow.

བཏང་ *(non-honorific)* བཏང་གནང་ *(honorific)*

བཏང་ (*past tense*)

1. ངས་ཁ་ས་གླིང་བུ་བཏང་པ་ཡིན།

   I played a flute yesterday.

2. ཁོང་གིས་ང་ལ་ཀུ་ཤུ་སྒམ་གང་བཏང་གནང་བྱུང་།

   He sent me a box of apples.

3. ཁོང་གིས་གྲོགས་མོ་ལ་ཡི་གེ་ཞིག་བཏང་གནང་སོང་།

   He sent a letter to his girl friend.

B) རྒྱག་ *(non-honorific)* ཀྱོན་ *(honorific)*

རྒྱག་ (*present tense*)

1. དེ་རིང་ཆར་པ་མང་པོ་རྒྱག་གི་འདུག

   Today, it's raining a lot.

2. ཁོང་ཁྲ་ཡོལ་རྒྱག་གི་འདུག

   He is hanging a window curtain.

3. ཟླ་བ་ལགས་ཆང་ས་རྒྱག་གི་འདུག

   Dawa la is getting married.

བརྒྱབ་ *(non-honorific)* བཀྱོན་ *(honorific)*

2. བརྒྱབ་ (*future tense*)

Examples :

1. སང་ཉིན་གངས་<u>བརྒྱབ་</u> / <u>འབབ་</u>ཀྱི་རེད།

It will snow tomorrow.

2. ང་དེ་རིང་སྐོར་ར་བརྒྱབ་ཀྱི་ཡིན།

Today, I will circumambulate.

3. ང་ཚོ་ཟླ་བ་གཅིག་གི་རིང་སྒོམ་བརྒྱབ་ཀྱི་ཡིན།

We will meditate for one month.

3. ཁོང་ཚོ་ཟླ་བ་འགའ་ཤས་སྒོམ་བཀྱོན་གནང་གི་རེད།

They will meditate for some months.

བརྒྱབ་ *(non-honorific)* བཀྱོན་ *(honorific)*

3. བརྒྱབ་ (*past tense*)

Examples :

1. ངས་ཁོང་ལ་ཁབ་བརྒྱབ་པ་ཡིན།

I gave an injection to you.

2. དེབ་འདི་དཔར་སློག་ཐེངས་གཉིས་བརྒྱབ་པ་རེད།

This book was reprinted twice.

3. ང་ཚོས་ཁ་སང་དགོང་དྲོ་ཞབས་བྲོ་བརྒྱབ་པ་ཡིན།

We danced yesterday evening.

4. ཁོང་གིས་ཞབས་བྲོ་མང་པོ་བརྒྱུན་སོང་།

She danced a lot.

C) བྱེད་ *(non-honorific)* བྱེད་གནང་ *(honorific)*

1. བྱེད་ (*present tense*)

1. ཁོང་གིས་ཁྱེད་རང་ལ་སྐྱོན་བརྗོད་གནང་གི་འདུག

He is criticising you.

2. ཁྱེད་རང་ཁོང་ཁྲོ་གནང་གི་འདུག

You are getting angry.

3. ང་ཅ་ལག་ལ་ཅག་ག་བྱེད་ཀྱི་ཡོད།

I am taking care of (my) things.

བྱེད་ *(non-honorific)* བྱེད་གནང་ *(honorific)*

2. བྱ་ / བྱེད་ (*future tense*)

1. ང་ལས་ཀ་བྱེད་པར་འགྲོ་གི་ཡིན།

I will go to work.

2. ཁོང་སྨན་བཅོས་གནང་བར་ཕེབས་ཀྱི་རེད།

He will go for medical treatment.

3. ཁྱེད་རང་ཁོང་མཇལ་བར་མ་ཕེབས་ན་ སྤྲུགས་འཁྲུལ་ གནང་གི་རེད།

She will be worried, if you don't go to see her.

3. བྱས་ (*past tense*)

1. ངོ་རྒོལ་བྱས་ protested

ང་ཚོས་རྒྱ་མི་ལ་ངོ་རྒོལ་བྱས་པ་ཡིན།

We have protested against the Chinese.

2. ཁོང་ཁྲོ་བྱས་ get angry

ཡིན་ནའང་། ང་ཚོས་རྒྱ་མི་ལ་ཁོང་ཁྲོ་བྱས་བྱས་མེད།

But we didn't get angry with the Chinese.

3. བསླབ་བྱ་བྱས་ advised

ང་ཚོས་ཁོང་ཚོར་བསླབ་བྱ་བྱས་པ་ཡིན།

We have advised them.

How to use དང་ (dang) in different method with different meanings :

I. དང་ *means "AND". It is used to separate two or more words :*

Examples :

1. ངས་ཀུ་ཤུ་ཁ་ཤས་དང་ ཚལ་ཉོས་པ་ཡིན།

I bought some apples and vegetables.

2. ང་ཨ་རི་དང་ དབྱིན་ཡུལ་དང་ ཉི་ཧོང་དང་ རྒྱ་གར་དང་ བལ་ཡུལ་ལ་ཕྱིན་པ་ཡིན།

I went to America, England, Japan, India and Nepal.

II. དང་ *Also indicates the cause & reason.*

Examples :

1. ཁོང་གིས་གསོལ་སྨན་མཆོད་པ་དང་སྐུ་གཞི་དྲག་སོང་།

He ate medicine and (*therefore*) was alright.

2. ངས་ཆང་བཏུངས་པ་དང་ར་བཟི་ཤག

I drank chang and (*therefore*) was drunk.

3. ངས་ཁ་དཔར་བཏང་པ་དང་ཁོང་ལམ་སང་ཐེབས་བྱུང་།

I telephoned him and (*therefore*) he came immediately.

III. དང་ *Also indicates the "time " (when)*

Examples :

1. ཉི་མ་ཤར་བ་དང་ང་ལས་ཀ་ལ་ཕྱིན་པ་ཡིན།

I went to work at sunrise.

2. ངས་སྒོ་ཕྱེ་བ་དང་ཁོང་ནང་ལ་འཛུལ་བྱུང་།

He/she entered the room when I opened the door.

IV. དང་ *Also indicates the "request" It also indicates "imperative mood"*

Examples :

1. ང་ལ་ཇ་དཀར་ཡོལ་གང་བཟོས་དང་།

Please make me a cup of tea.

2. ཕྱག་དེབ་འདི་སྤུས་གཟིགས་གནང་དང་།

Please buy this book.

3. ཁོང་ལ་ཕྱག་རོགས་གནང་དང་།

Please help him.

4 གཟིགས་དང་། Look !

THE USE OF པ་ (PA), པོ་ (PO), བ་ (WA) & པ་ (PA) WITH DIFFERENT NOUNS AND COMPARATIVES :

Nouns and adjectives always use པ་ *(pa)* or པོ་ *(po)* after the suffixes ending with ག་ ད་ ན་ བ་ མ་ས་ and post suffix ད་

With exception of the feminine particles མ་ *(ma)* & མོ་ *(mo)*.

Examples with པ་ *(pa)*:

1. འབྲོག་པ། nomad.

   ཁོང་འབྲོག་པ་རེད།

   He/she is a nomad.

2. བོད་པ། Tibetan

   ང་ཚོ་བོད་པ་ཡིན།

   We are Tibetans.

3. ལམ་སྟོན་པ། adviser

   ཁོང་ང་ཚོའི་ལམ་སྟོན་པ་རེད།

   He is our adviser

4. སྲབ་པ། thinner *(of things only)*

དེབ་འདི་ལས་དེ་སྲབ་པ་འདུག

This book is thinner than that book.

5. རོགས་རམ་པ། sponsor

ང་ཚོའི་སློབ་གྲྭ་ལ་རོགས་རམ་པ་འགའ་ཤས་ཡོད།

Our school has some sponsors.

6. ཕྱིན་པ། went

ཁོང་དབྱིན་ཡུལ་ལ་ཕྱིན་པ་རེད།

He/she went to England.

7. ཆོས་པ། a Dharma practitioner

ཁོང་ཆོས་པ་རེད།

He/she is a Dharma practitioner.

Examples with པོ་ (po)

1. ཕྱུག་པོ་ rich

རྡོ་རྗེ་ལགས་ ཕྱུག་པོ་མ་རེད།

Dorjee is not a rich (man).

2. རྒོད་པོ། high spirited / wild

བུ་འདི་རྒོད་པོ་ཞི་དྲག་འདུག

This boy is very wild or high spirited.

3. དཔོན་པོ། leader / head

ཁྱེད་རང་ང་ཚོའི་དཔོན་པོ་རེད།

You are our leader.

4. སྲབ་པོ། thin *(of things only)*

རས་འདི་སྲབ་པོ་ཞི་དྲག་འདུག

This cloth is very fine or thin.

5. འཇམ་པོ། soft

བལ་འདི་འཇམ་པོ་མི་འདུག

This wool is not soft.

6. མཁས་པོ། expert / skilful

ཁོང་གློག་བཟོ་མཁས་པོ་ཡོག་རེད།

He is an expert at fixing electrical things.

བ་ *(WA)* AND པ་ *(PA)* ARE USED AFTER THE SUFFIXES ང་ འ་ ར་ ལ་ & མཐའ་མེད་ (*an independent root letter without suffix*)

According to the grammarian Yangchen Dup-pai Dorjee, it's recommended that བ་(*wa*) is used with odd number and པ་ (*pa*) is used with even numbers.

Examples with བ་ (wa):

1. རྒྱལ་ཚོང་བ། traitor
   ཁོང་ཚོ་རྒྱལ་ཚོང་བ་མ་རེད།
   They are not traitors.

2. ཟློས་གར་བ། performer
   བོད་ཀྱི་ཟློས་གར་བ་འགའ་ཤས་དབྱིན་ཡུལ་ལ་ཕྱིན་པ་རེད།
   Some Tibetan performers went to England.

3. གསང་སྐུལ་བ། spy
   རྒྱ་མིའི་གསང་སྐུལ་བ་ཞིག་བོད་ལ་སླེབས་པ་རེད།
   A Chinese spy came to Tibet.

4. ཁ་ལོ་བ། driver

ཁོང་ང་ཚོའི་ཁ་ལོ་བ་རེད།

He is our driver.

5. གསེར་བཟོ་བ། goldsmith

ཁོང་གསེར་བཟོ་བ་རེད།

He is a goldsmith.

6. ལྷ་ས་བ། a person from Lhasa

ཁོང་ལྷ་ས་བ་རེད།

She is from Lhasa.

Examples with པ་ (*pa*) :

1. ཚོང་པ། businessman

ཁོང་ཚོང་པ་ཆེན་པོ་ཞིག་རེད།

He is a big businessman.

2. མདའ་པ། archer

ཁོང་མདའ་པ་རེད།

He is an archer.

3. གར་པ། dancer

ཁོང་གར་པ་མ་རེད།

He/she is not a dancer.

4. འགྲུལ་པ། traveller

ཁོང་ཚོ་འགྲུལ་པ་རེད།

They are travellers.

5. གྲྭ་པ། monk

ཁོང་ཚོ་སེ་རའི་གྲྭ་པ་རེད།

They are Sera monks.

Use of མ་ *(ma)* & མོ་ *(mo)*

The feminime བདག་སྒྲ་ *(categorical particle)* མ་*(ma) &* མོ་ *(mo) are not governed by any of the rules. This occurs whenever the feminine gender is to be indicated.*

Examples :

བོད་མོ་ a Tibetan woman

ཁམས་མོ་	(a) woman from Kham province
ཆང་མ་	beer woman *(beer maker or seller)*
ཇ་མ་	tea woman *(tea maker)*
འབྲོག་མོ་	nomad *(female)*

The negative particle " མ་ " (ma) is sometimes inserted into certain types of compound words to modify the meaning.

Examples :

གངས་མ་ཆར་	*"not - snow - not - rain "*	*(slush)*
ར་མ་ལུག་	*"not - goat - not - sheep "*	*(mixture)*

ཕོ་མོའི་དབྱེ་བ། Masculine & Feminine Gender

In general, nouns that are the names of males are said to be the Masculine Gender and nouns that are the names of female are said to be the Feminine Gender.

Let us study some of the nouns that indicate the names of male and female persons.

Masculine		Feminine	
ལྷ་	God	ལྷ་མོ་	Goddess
གྲྭ་པ་	monk	བཙུན་མ་/ཨ་ནེ་	nun
རྒྱལ་པོ་	king	བཙུན་མོ་	queen
སྲས་	prince	སྲས་མོ་	princess
སློབ་སྟོན་པ་	instructor	སློབ་སྟོན་མ	instructress
ཕོ་ཧྲང་	batchelor	མོ་ཧྲང་	spinster
བུ་	boy / son	བུ་མོ་	daughter / girl
གཅེན་པོ་	elder brother	གཅེན་མོ་	elder sister
གཅུང་པོ་	younger brother	གཅུང་མོ་	younger sister
གཡོག་པོ་	man- servant	གཡོག་མོ་	maid -servant
ཁྱོ་ག་	husband	ཆུང་མ་	wife

Masculine		Feminine	
སྐྱེས་པ་	man	བུད་མེད་	woman
ཚ་བོ་	nephew	ཚ་མོ་	niece
པ་ཕ་	father	ཨ་མ་	mother
འབྲོག་པ་	nomad	འབྲོག་མོ་	nomad (female)
དབུས་པ་	man from central province	དབུས་མོ་	woman from central province

These are some of the nouns which indicate the names of male and female animals :

Masculine		Feminine	
བྱ་ཕོ་	cock	བྱ་མོ་	hen
ཕག་པ་	pig	ཕག་མོ་	sow
ར་ཕོ་	goat (male)	ར་མོ་	goat (female)
གླང་	bull	བ་མོ་	cow
ཁྱི་	dog	ཁྱི་མོ་	bitch
སྟག་	tiger	སྟག་མོ་	tigress

Use of ན་ (na)

ན་ which means " if " or " unless "

Examples :

1. སྙན་ཞུ་འདི་མ་ཕུལ་ན་ཡག་པོ་ཡོག་མ་རེད།

It's not good, unless the petition is presented.

2. ཡི་གེ་འདི་མ་བྲིས་ན་ཡག་པོ་ཡོག་མ་རེད།

It's not good, unless (you) write this letter.

3. དེབ་འདི་བཀློགས་ན་ཡག་པོ་ཡོག་རེད།

It will be good, if (you) read this book.

4. ཁྱེད་རང་བོད་ལ་ཕྱིན་ན་ཡག་པོ་ཡོག་རེད།

It would be good, if you went to Tibet.

Use of དགོས་ (goe) :

དགོས་ means " want ", " need, " " have to " & " has to ".

A དགོས་ " want or need "

དགོས་ is used in the literary form and དགོ་ is used in the colloquial.

Examples :

1. ང་ལ་ཆུ་གྲང་མོ་མི་དགོས། *(written)*

   I don't want cold water.

2. ང་ལ་ཚ་ལུ་མ་དགོ *(spoken)*

   I want an orange.

3. ང་ཚོ་ལ་ཁང་མིག་འགའ་ཤས་དགོས་ཀྱི་འདུག *(written)*

   We wants some rooms.

B དགོས་ *" have to or has to"*

1. ང་ཁྲོམ་ནས་ཚལ་ཉོ་དགོས་ཡོད། (*written*)

   I have to buy vegetables from the market.

2. ང་ཚོ་བོད་ལ་འགྲོ་དགོ་ཡོད། (*spoken*)

   We have to go to Tibet.

3. ཁྱེད་རང་ལྡི་ལི་ལ་ཕེབས་དགོས་རེད། (*written*)

   You have to go to Delhi.

4. ཁོང་ཚོགས་འདུ་ལ་ཕེབས་དགོ་རེད། (*spoken*)

   He has to go for a meeting.

USAGE OF ནས་ & ལས་ WHICH COMES UNDER THE ABLATIVE CASE.

A ནས་ (nas) & ལས་ (las) means *"from"* refering to the sourse or origin.

Examples :

1. འོ་མ་བ་ནས་འབྱུང་བ་རེད།
   འོ་མ་བ་ལས་འབྱུང་བ་རེད།
   Milk comes from (a) cow.
2. བཟོ་གྲྭ་ནས་དཀར་ཡོལ་འབྱུང་བ་རེད།
   བཟོ་གྲྭ་ལས་དཀར་ཡོལ་འབྱུང་བ་རེད།
   Cups comes from the factory.
3. ཤིང་སྡོང་ནས་ཤིང་ཏོག་འབྱུང་བ་རེད།
   ཤིང་སྡོང་ལས་ཤིང་ཏོག་འབྱུང་བ་རེད།
   Fruits comes from the tree.

In colloquial Tibetan ནས་ *(nas)* is used often instead of ལས་ *(las).*

B ནས་ *(nas)* is also used to compare and contrast similar things .

Examples :

1. བོད་ཀྱི་སེམས་ཅན་ནང་ནས་གཡག་ཡག་ཤོས་འདུག

" Amongst the animals of Tibet, the yak is the best,"

i.e. Yak is better than (all) other animals.

2. ཟ་ཁང་གི་ནང་ནས་གཡག་ཟ་ཁང་ཡག་ག་འདུག

" Among restaurants, the yak restaurant is better,"

i.e. The yak restaurant is better than (all) other restaurants.

C ནས་ which means "*from*"

1. ང་ཁྲོམ་ནས་ཡོང་པ་ཡིན།

I came from the market.

2. ཡི་གེ་འདི་བོད་ནས་བཏང་པ་རེད།

This letter was sent from Tibet.

3. དེབ་འདི་བོད་ཀྱི་དཔེ་མཛོད་ཁང་ནས་དཔར་བསྒྲུན་པ་རེད།

This book is published by the Library of Tibetan works & Archives.

D ནས་ sometimes indicates "*and*" in colloquial Tibetan, when it's used with a verb.

1. ཁོང་གསོལ་ཇ་མཆོད་ཚར་ནས་ཁྲོམ་ལ་ཐེག་གི་རེད།

   We will finish the tea and go to the market.

2. ང་ཁྲོམ་ལ་ཕྱིན་ནས་ཚལ་ཏོག་ཙམ་ཉོ་གི་ཡིན།

   I will go to the market and buy some vegetables.

3. ངས་དེབ་འདི་ཉོས་ནས་ཁོང་ལ་འབུལ་གྱི་ཡིན།

   I will buy this book and give (it) to him.

Use of the ལས་ *(las)*

A ལས་ " Karma "

Examples :

1. དེ་ཁྱེད་རང་གི་ལས་རེད།

   That's your karma.

2. ལས་ནི་མི་བསླུ་བ་རེད།

   The karma is infallible.

B ལས་ is also used in comparative.

Examples :

1. གཡག་ལས་གླང་ཆེན་ཆེ་བ་འདུག

The elephant is bigger than the yak.

2. ཇ་ལས་འོ་མ་ཞིམ་པ་འདུག

Milk is tastier than tea.

1. ཞི་མི་ལས་ཙི་ཙི་ཆུང་བ་འདུག

The mouse is smaller than the cat.

2. མི་ལས་རྟ་མགྱོགས་པ་འདུག

Horses are faster than men.

མང་ཚིག

Plurals

I The below mentioned pronouns & demonstrative pronouns form their plurals by adding ཚོ་ *(tso)* to the singular.

Singular		Plural	
ང་	I	ང་ཚོ་	we
ཁྱེད་	you	ཁྱེད་ཚོ་	you
ཁྱེད་རང་	you	ཁྱེད་རང་ཚོ་	you *(plural)*
ཁོ་	he	ཁོ་ཚོ་	they
ཁོང་	he/she	ཁོང་ཚོ་	they (h) **
ཕ་གི་ **	that	ཕ་ཚོ་	those
དེ་ *	that	དེ་ཚོ་	those

ཕ་གི་ ** "that" the object should be visible from a distance.

དེ་* "that" Not necessary to see the object.

(h) ** honorific

II These nouns form their plural by adding ཚོ་ *(tso)* to the singular. This is used only for people.

Singular		Plural	
བུ་	boy	བུ་ཚོ་	boys
བུ་མོ་	girl	བུ་མོ་ཚོ་	girls
ཁྱོ་ག་	man	ཁྱོ་ག་ཚོ་	men
བུད་མེད་	woman	བུད་མེད་ཚོ་	women
མ་བྱན་	cook	མ་བྱན་ཚོ་	cooks
ཚོང་པ་	businessman	ཚོང་པ་ཚོ་	businessmen
ཞིང་པ	farmer	ཞིང་པ་ཚོ་	farmers
འབྲོག་པ་	nomad	འབྲོག་པ་ཚོ	nomads
ནང་མི་	family	ནང་མི་ཚོ	families
ཤིང་བཟོ་བ	carpenter	ཤིང་བཟོ་བ་ཚོ་	carpenters

III Most of the nouns and things form their plural by adding དེ་ཚོ་ *(those) or* འདི་ཚོ་ *(these)* to the singular.

Singular		Plural	
དེབ་	book	དེབ་འདི་ཚོ་	These books

ཁང་པ	house	ཁང་པ་དེ་ཚོ་	those houses
ཁང་མིག་	room	ཁང་མིག་ འདི་ཚོ་	these rooms
སྒོ་	door	སྒོ་འདི་ཚོ་	these doors
སྨྱུ་གུ་	pen	སྨྱུ་གུ་འདི་ཚོ་	these pens
རྐུ་མ་	thief	རྐུ་མ་དེ་ཚོ་	those thieves
རྟ་	horse	རྟ་དེ་ཚོ་	those horses
སྤྲེའུ་	monkey	སྤྲེའུ་འདི་ཚོ་	these monkeys
ལྡེ་མིག་	key	ལྡེ་མིག་འདི་ཚོ་	these keys

IV These nouns form their plurals by adding words like མང་པོ་ *(many)*, མང་པོ་ཞི་དྲག་ *(a lot of)*, འགའ་ཤས་ *(some)*, འདི་ཚོ་ *(these)* , དེ་ཚོ་ *(those)* and a definate number (more than one) to the singular.

Singular		Plural	
ཆུ་ཚོད་	watch / hour	ཆུ་ཚོད་མང་པོ་	many watches/ hours
ཡལ་ག་	branch	ཡལ་ག་མང་པོ་ཞི་དྲག་	a lot of branches
གླང་ཆེན་	elephant	གླང་ཆེན་ལྔ་	five elephants
ཕག་པ་	pig	ཕག་པ་འགའ་ཤས་	some pigs
ལུག་	sheep	ལུག་མང་པོ་	many sheeps

ཤ་བ་	deer	ཤ་བ་གསུམ་	three deers
ཉ་	fish	ཉ་མང་པོ་ཞི་དྲག་	a lot of fish
བ་ཕྱུགས་	cow	བ་ཕྱུགས་ཁ་ཤས་	some cows

Observe how the above mentioned nouns, pronouns and demonstrative pronouns form their plurals :

(I)

1. ང་དེབ་ཀློག་གི་ཡིན། I will read (a) book.

   ང་ཚོ་དེབ་ཀློག་གི་ཡིན། We will read books.

2. ཁྱེད་རང་བལ་ཡུལ་ལ་ཐེག་གི་རེད།

   You will go to Nepal.

   ཁྱེད་རང་ཚོ་བལ་ཡུལ་ལ་ཐེག་གི་རེད།

   You (pl.) will go to Nepal.

3. ཁོང་བོད་པ་རེད། He/she is a Tibetan.

   ཁོང་ཚོ་བོད་པ་རེད། They are Tibetans.

4. པ་གི་སྟག་རེད། That is a tiger.

པ་ཚོ་སྟག་རེད། Those are tigers.

5. དེ་ཁྱི་རེད། That is a dog.

དེ་ཚོ་ཁྱི་རེད། Those are dogs.

6. འདི་ངའི་དེབ་རེད། This is my book.

འདི་ཚོ་ངའི་དེབ་རེད། These are my books.

(II)

1. བུ་མོ་སློབ་གྲྭ་ལ་ཐེག་གི་འདུག

The girl is going to the school.

བུ་མོ་ཚོ་སློབ་གྲྭར་ཐེག་གི་འདུག

The girls are going to the school.

2. ཚོང་པ་དེ་གསོལ་ཇ་མཆོད་ཀྱི་འདུག

The businessman is drinking tea.

ཚོང་པ་དེ་ཚོ་ཉིན་གུང་ཞལ་ལག་མཆོད་ཀྱི་འདུག

The businessmen are eating lunch.

3. ཤིང་བཟོ་བ་ཕ་གི་ཞབས་བཀྱག་བཟོ་གནང་གི་འདུག

That carpenter is making chair.

ཤིང་བཟོ་བ་ཚོ་ཞབས་བཀྱག་བཟོ་གནང་གི་འདུག

The carpenters are making chairs.

(III)

1. འདི་དེབ་རེད།	འདི་ཚོ་དེབ་རེད།
This is (a) book.	These are books.

2. ལྡེ་མིག་འདི་ཚེ་རིང་ལགས་ལ་གནང་རོགས་གནང་།

Please give this key to Tsering la.

ལྡེ་མིག་འདི་ཚོ་ཚེ་རིང་ལགས་ལ་གནང་རོགས་གནང་།

Please give these keys to Tsering la.

3. ཁང་མིག་འདི་ངའི་རེད།	ཁང་མིག་དེ་ཚོ་ང་ཚོའི་རེད།
That is my room.	Those are our rooms.
4. རྟ་འདི་ཡག་པོ་འདུག	རྟ་འདི་ཚོ་ཡག་པོ་འདུག
This is a good horse.	These are good horses.

(IV)

1. ཞིང་ཁའི་ནང་ལ་ལུག་ཅིག་འདུག

   There is a sheep in the field.

   ཞིང་ཁའི་ནང་ལ་ལུག་མང་པོ་འདུག

   There are many sheep in the field.

2. ངས་རིའི་སྒང་ལ་ཤ་བ་ཞིག་མཐོང་བྱུང་།

   I saw a deer on the mountain.

   ངས་རིའི་སྒང་ལ་ཤ་བ་ལྔ་མཐོང་བྱུང་།

   I saw five deer on the mountain.

3. ང་ཚོས་ཆུ་ཚོད་ཅིག་ཉོས་པ་ཡིན།

   We bought a watch.

   ང་ཚོས་ཆུ་ཚོད་ཁ་ཤས་ཉོས་པ་ཡིན།

   We bought some watches.

4. ཁོང་གིས་ཆུའི་ནང་ལ་ཉ་ཞིག་མཐོང་འདུག

   He saw a fish in the water.

   ཁོང་གིས་ཆུའི་ནང་ལ་ཉ་མང་པོ་ཞི་དྲག་མཐོང་འདུག

   She saw a lot of fish in the water.

རྣམས། (n̄am)

The function of the རྣམས་ is exactly the same as ཚོ་ (tso).

ཚོ་ (tso) is used in the colloquial and རྣམས་ (n̄am) is used in the literary form. In general it is possible to replace the ཚོ་ (tso) with རྣམས (n̄am) to make the plural.

Examples:

ཕྲུག་གུ་རྣམས་སློབ་གྲྭར་ཕེབས་སོང་།

Children went to school.

ཞིང་པ་རྣམས་སྤྲོ་སྐྱིད་ལ་ཕེབས་གནང་གི་འདུག

Farmers are going for the picnic.

འབྲོག་པ་རྣམས་འོ་མ་བཞེས་གི་འདུག

Nomads are taking milk.

རྣམ་པ་ (n̄am-pa)

The function of the རྣམ་པ་ is also the same as ཚོ་ (tso) and རྣམས (n̄am) but རྣམ་པ་ (n̄am-pa) is used with the pronouns of first, second and third persons.

Examples:

1. ང་རང་རྣམ་པ་ we
2. ཁྱེད་རྣམ་པ་ you (plural)
3. ཁྱེད་རང་རྣམ་པ་ you (plural)
4. ཁོང་རྣམ་པ་ they

The plural sign རྣམ་པ་ is also used with all kinds of nouns which indicate persons.

Examples:

1. དགེ་འདུན་པ་རྣམ་པ་ monks
2. དགེ་རྒན་རྣམ་པ་ teachers
3. སློབ་ཕྲུག་རྣམ་པ་ students
4. ཕ་མ་རྣམ་པ་ parents
5. སྐྱ་མགྲོན་རྣམ་པ་ guests

Use of ཡག་ རྒྱུ་ & ག་ The Infinitivies

The indefinate particle རྒྱུ་(gyu), ཡག་(yag) and ག་(ga) have the function of "TO".

I) རྒྱུ་(gyu)

In general རྒྱུ་(gyu) is used in the lilerary form but it is also used in the spoken language. Such as :

1. ཕེབས་རྒྱུ་ to go or come
2. བཏུང་རྒྱུ་ to drink
3. མཆོད་རྒྱུ་ to drink and eat
4. མཇུག་གུ་བསྐྱལ་རྒྱུ་ to be completed

These indefinate particles are used with all kinds of verbs.

Examples:

1. ཁོང་གིས་ཕྱག་ལས་དེ་མཇུག་གུ་བསྐྱལ་རྒྱུ་རེད།

   His work is to be completed.

2. ང་ཞོགས་ཇ་བཏུང་རྒྱུ་ཡིན།

   I have to eat (my) breakfast.

3. ཁོང་ད་ལྟ་ལྡི་ལི་ལ་ཐོན་རྒྱུ་རེད།

   He is just about to leave for Delhi.

4. ཁོང་ཚོ་ཉིན་གུང་གསོལ་ཚིགས་མཆོད་རྒྱུ་རེད།

II) ཡག་ *(yag)*

The infinitive particle ཡག་ *(yag)* is used in the colloquial Tibetan and have the function of " To ".

Examples :

1. ཡི་གེ་དེ་བོད་ལ་གཏོང་ཡག་རེད།

   That letter is to be sent to Tibet.

2. ཆུ་འདི་བཏུང་ཡག་མ་རེད།

   This water is not for drinking.

3. ཤིང་འདི་ཞབས་བཀྱག་བཟོ་ཡག་རེད།

   This wood is to make (a) chair.

4. ཅ་ལག་དེ་ཚོ་ཚོང་ཡག་རེད།

   Those things are not for sale.

III) ག་ *(ga)* བར་ *(war)* and པར་ *(par)*

The infinitive particle ག་ *(ga)* is used only in spoken and བར་ *(war)* / པར་ *(par)* are used in written form. These three infinifives are used with verbs like ཡོང་ (come), བཅར་ (come & go), འགྲོ་ (go), ཕེབས་ (come & go) and ཕྱིན་ (went) which express the purpose of *going and coming*. Some of the examples showing how the infinitive (ga) is used in spoken and པར་ (par) / བར་ (war) in written form.

1. ང་ལྡི་ལི་ལ་སློབ་སྦྱོང་བྱེད་ག་ཡོང་གི་ཡིན། *spoken*
ང་ལྡི་ལི་ལ་སློབ་སྦྱོང་བྱེད་པར་ཡོང་གི་ཡིན། *written*
I will come to Delhi to study.

2. ང་ཁོང་གི་སར་ཡི་གེ་འབུལ་ག་བཅར་གྱི་ཡིན། *spoken*
ང་ཁོང་གི་སར་ཡི་གེ་འབུལ་བར་བཅར་གྱི་ཡིན *written*
I will go to his place to deliver a letter.

3. ཟླ་བ་ལགས་ཁྱེད་རང་མཇལ་ག་བཅར་གྱི་རེད། *(s)*
ཟླ་བ་ལགས་ཁྱེད་རང་མཇལ་བར་བཅར་གྱི་རེད *(w)*
Dawa la will come to see you.

4. ཁོང་ཁྲོམ་ལ་ཚལ་གཟིགས་ག་ཕེབས་སོང་། *spoken*
ཁོང་ཁྲོམ་ལ་ཚལ་གཟིགས་པར་ཕེབས་སོང་། *written*
He went to the market to buy (some) vegetables.

Note: The verb བཅར་ = "go " "come" is actually honorific. Nevertheless it can be used by oneself i.e. "I" , when one is showing respect for another.

For example :

ང་བཅར་གྱི་ཡིན། I will come / go.

ང་ཁྱེད་རང་སར་བཅར་གྱི་ཡིན།

I will come to your place.

ང་ཁོང་གི་སར་བཅར་གྱི་ཡིན།

I will go to his/her place.

ང་ཁྱེད་རང་མཉམ་དུ་བཅར་གྱི་ཡིན།

I will come / go with you.

---

* གཟིགས་ " to buy " " to see "

When the letter བ་ (ba) appears as a part of a word in the following nouns, verbs & comparatives, it is always pronounced "WA".

- **Examples :**

1.	ཀོ་བ་	(ko-wa)	leather
2.	ཀ་བ་	(ka-wa)	pillar
3.	ཁ་བ་	(kha-wa)	snow
4.	ཚ་བ་	(tsha-wa)	heat, fever & temperature
5.	དུ་བ་	(du-wa)	smoke
6.	ཤ་བ་	(sha-wa)	deer
7.	ལྟེ་བ་	(te-wa)	main / navel
8.	ཉལ་བ་	(nyal-wa)	to sleep
9.	ཉོ་བ་	(nyo-wa)	to buy
10.	ཆེ་བ་	(che-wa)	bigger
11.	ཆུང་བ་	(chung-wa)	smaller
12.	མང་བ་	(mang-wa)	more etc.

ལྡོག་ཕྱོགས། **Opposites**

ཆེན་པོ་	big	ཆུང་ཆུང་	small
རིང་པོ་	long	ཐུང་ཐུང་	short
གོང་ཆེན་པོ་	expensive	གོང་ཆུང་ཆུང་	cheap
ཚ་པོ་	hot	གྲང་མོ་	cold
ཡག་པོ་	good	སྡུག་ཅག་	bad
བུ་	boy/son	བུ་མོ་	girl/daughter
ཁྱོ་ག་	man	བུད་མེད་	woman
ཉིན་	day	མཚན་	night
རྒྱག་པ་	fat	སྐམ་པོ་	thin (of person & animals)
ལྗིད་པོ། ལྗི་བ་	heavy	ཡང་པོ་	light
གཙང་མ་	clean	བཙོག་པ། རྫོར་པོ་	dirty
གསར་པ་	new	རྙིང་པ་	old
མངར་མོ་	sweet	སྐྱུར་མོ་	sour
མང་པོ་	many	ཉུང་ཉུང་	few
སྔ་པོ་	early	ཕྱི་པོ་	late
སྐྱོ་པོ་	poor	ཕྱུག་པོ་	rich
མཐུག་པོ་	thick	སྲབ་པོ་	thin (of things only)
མགྱོགས་པོ་	fast	འགོར་པོ་	slow

གཞོན་གཞོན་	young	རྒན་ཁོག་	old
དགའ་པོ། སྐྱིད་པོ་	happy	སྡུག་པོ་	sad
ཐག་རིང་པོ་	far	ཉེ་པོ་	close
ལས་སླ་པོ་	easy	ཁག་པོ་	difficult
གྲུང་པོ་	active	ཉོབ་པོ་	lazy
སྤྱང་པོ་	clever	ལྐུགས་པ་	foolish
བཟང་པོ་	noble / good	ངན་པ་	bad (not used for things)
སློ་ཁོག་ཆེན་པོ་	brave	སློ་ཁོག་ཆུང་ཆུང	coward
ཤུགས་ཆེན་པོ་	strong	ཤུགས་ཆུང་ཆུང་	weak

རྗེས་འཇུག་ ད་ ན་ ལ་ ས་ སོགས་ལ་དབྱངས་དང་
མིང་གཞིའི་ཡི་གེ་སྦྱར་བའི་སྒྲ

Sounds of the suffixes ད་ ན་ ལ་ ས་ with the root letters & vowel signs :

A 1. If the suffix ད་ (da) is used with any root letter, the sound will be ཨད་ (ä̀).

Examples :

སྐད། གད། ཚད། ནད། etc.

2. If the vowel sign " ི " (i) is used on a root letter with the suffix ད་ (da), the sound will be ཨིད་ (è).

Examples :

ཉིད། ཡིད། དཔྱིད། ཞྀད། etc.

3. If the vowel sign " ུ " (u) is used below a root letter with the suffix ད་ (da), the sound will be ཨུད་ (ǜ).

Examples :

རྩུད། ཡུད། རྡུད། སྐུད། etc.

4. If the vowel sign " ེ " (e) is used on a root letter with the suffix ད་ (da), the sound will be ཨེད་ (e`).

Examples :

རེད། མེད། ཆེད། པེད། etc.

5. If the vowel sign " ོ " (o) is used on a root letter with the suffix ད་ (da), the sound will be ཨོད་ (ö`).

Examples :

ཡོད། བོད། ཕོད། པོད། etc.

B 1. If the suffix ན་ (na) is used with any root letter, the sound will be ཨན་ (ä; n).

Examples :

མཁན། ཕན། གདན། གསན། etc.

2. If the vowel sign " ི " (i) is used on a root letter with the suffix ན་ (na), the sound will be ཨིན་ (i; n).

Examples :

ཉིན། མིན། ཟིན། ཡིན། etc.

3. If the vowel sign " ུ " (u) is used below a root letter with the suffix ན་ (na), the sound will be ཨུན་ (ü; n).

Examples :

ཀུན། ཐུན། ཚུན། ཕུན། etc.

4. If the vowel sign " ེ " (e) is used on a root letter with the suffix ན་ (na), the sound will be ཨེན་ (e ; n).

Examples :

ཆེན། ཉེན། ཐེན། ལེན། etc.

5. If the vowel sign " ོ " (o) is used on a root letter with the suffix ན་ (na), the sound will be ཨོན་ (ö; n).

Examples :

ཆོན། ཉོན། སྤོན། ལོན། etc.

C 1. If the suffix ལ་ (la) is used with any root letter, the sound will be ཨའི་ (ä:).

Examples :

བལ། གལ། ངལ། ཉལ། etc.

2. If the vowel sign " ི " (i) is used on a root letter with the suffix ལ་ (la), the sound will be ཨིའི་ (i:).

Examples :

སིལ། ཟིལ། རིལ། དྲིལ། etc.

3. If the vowel sign " ུ " (u) is used below a root letter with the suffix ལ་ (la), the sound will be ཨུའི་ (ü:).

Examples :

ཁུལ། ཕུལ། ཚུལ། ཡུལ། etc.

4. If the vowel sign " ེ " (e) is used on a root letter with the suffix ལ་ (la), the sound will be ཨེའི་ (e:).

Examples :

ཤེལ། སྤེལ། འཕེལ། སེལ། etc.

5. If the vowel sign " ོ " (o) is used on a root letter with the suffix ལ་ (la), the sound will be ཨོའི་ (ö:).

Examples :

ཚོལ། ཉོལ། མོལ། རོལ། etc.

D 1. If the suffix ས་ (sa) is used with any root letter, the sound will be ཨས་ (ä`).

Examples :

པས། གས། ངས། ཆས། etc.

2. If the vowel sign " ི " (i) is used on a root letter with the suffix ས་(sa), the sound will be ཨིས་ (i`).

Examples :

གིས། མིས། ཡིས། ཤིས། etc.

3. If the vowel sign " ུ " (u) is used below a root letter with the suffix ས་(sa), the sound will be ཨུས་ (ü`).

Examples :

དུས། ནུས། སུས། ཕུས། etc.

4. If the vowel sign " ེ " (e) is used on a root letter with the suffix ས་(sa), the sound will be ཨེས་ (e`).

Examples :

ངེས། ཅེས། དེས། ཉེས། etc.

5. If the vowel sign " ོ " (o) is used on a root letter with the suffix ས་(sa), the sound will be ཨོས་ (ö`).

Examples :

ཁོས། གོས། ཆོས། ཉོས། etc.

ཤད་བེད་སྤྱོད་བྱེད་སྟངས།

How to use vertical slashes [ཤད་] in different situations :

I གཅིག་ཤད། (a single vertical slash)

A single vertical slash [ཤད་] is used after a sentence. This indicates the full-stop in English.

Examples :

1. ང་ལ་ལྡུམ་ར་ཆུང་ཆུང་ཞིག་ཡོད།

   I have a small garden.

2 ཁོང་ངའི་ཨ་མ་ལགས་རེད།

She is my mother.

3. ང་རྡོ་རྗེ་ཚེ་རིང་ཡིན།

I am Dorjee Tsering.

II A single vertical slash [ཤད་] is also used to separate the numbers and nouns etc. (Like a comma in English)

Exam ples :

1. ངས་བོད་དང་། རྒྱ་གར། དབྱིན་ཡུལ། བལ་ཡུལ་ སོགས་ལ་ཕྱིན་པ་ཡིན།

   I went to Tibet, India, England and Nepal.

2. གཅིག གཉིས། གསུམ། བཞི། བཅུ། ལྟ་བུ།

   one, two, three, four, & ten.

III གཉིས་ཤད། (two vertical slashes)

Two vertical slashes [ཤད་] are used after each line of a poem.

Example :

མཁས་པ་སློབ་པའི་དུས་ན་འདུག།
བདེ་བར་སྡོད་ལ་མཁས་མི་སྲིད།།
བདེ་བ་ཆུང་ལ་ཆགས་པ་དེས།།
ཆེན་པོའི་བདེ་བ་ཐོབ་མི་སྲིད།།

Two vertical slashes [ཤད་] are also used after the completion of a thought but when a line of verse or sentence ends in the suffix ག་ (ga), a single vertical slash (shad) is used instead of two slashes. This is because the vertical stroke of the suffix ག་ (ga) is counted as a vertical slash [ཤད་].

IV བཞི་ཤད། (four vertical slashes)

Four vertical slashes [ཤད་] are used at the end of a chapter or to close a long passage of prose.

Exceptions : In general when the vertical slashes [ཤད] are used, the dot (tseg) is omitted but for the suffix ང་ (nga) a dot (tseg) is necessary before a ཤད་ (shad) . The reason for this is because if a vertical slash is used right after the letter ང་ (nga), it might look like the letter བ (ba).

Examples :

1. ང་ལ་ཁ་སླ་ཡི་གེ་ཞིག་འབྱོར་བྱུང་།

   Yesterday I received a letter.

2. ཁོང་ངའི་སར་ཕེབས་བྱུང་།

   He /she came to my place.

A SELECTED LIST OF VERBS WHICH ARE OFTEN USED IN THE SPOKEN LANGUAGE

Verbs in the three tenses with imperative:

དོན་དག་ *Meanings*	མ་འོངས་པ་ *Future*	ད་ལྟ་བ་ *Present*	འདས་པ་ *Past*	སྐུལ་ཚིག་ *Imperative*
to listen	ཉན་	ཉན་	ཉན་	ཉོན་
to tell	ལབ་	ལབ་	ལབ་	ལོབ་ཅིག
to come	ཡོང་	ཡོང་	ཡོང་	***
to squeeze	བཙིར་	བཙིར་	བཙིར་	བཙིར་ཅིག
to be late	འགོར་	འགོར་	འགོར་	***
to sleep	ཉལ་	ཉལ་	ཉལ་	ཉོལ་ཅིག
to receive /arrive	འབྱོར་	འབྱོར་	འབྱོར་	***
to see	མཐོང་	མཐོང་	མཐོང་	***
to borrow/ lend	གཡར་	གཡར་	གཡར་	གཡོར་ཅིག
to meet	ཐུག་	ཐུག་	ཐུག་	ཐུག་ཅིག
to wear	གྱོན་	གྱོན་	གྱོན་	གྱོན་ཅིག་
to catch	ཟིན་	ཟིན་	ཟིན་	ཟུང་ཤིག

to know	ཤེས་	ཤེས་	ཤེས་	***
to fly	འཕུར་	འཕུར་	འཕུར་	འཕུར་ཅིག
to remember	ངེས་	ངེས་	ངེས་	***
to remember	དྲན་	དྲན་	དྲན་	དྲན་ཅིག
to leave	ཐོན་	ཐོན་	ཐོན་	ཐོན་ཅིག
to touch	རེག་	རེག་	རེག་	རེག་ཅིག
to put	ལྡུག་	ལྡུག་	ལྡུག་	ལྡུགས་ཤིག
(something in a container)				
to eat/ drink (h)	བཞེས་	བཞེས་	བཞེས་	བཞེས་ཤིག
to pull	འཐེན་	འཐེན་	འཐེན་	འཐེན་ཅིག
to see / meet (h)	མཇལ་	མཇལ་	མཇལ་	མཇོལ་ཅིག

Note: *The future, present, & past remain the same in the above.*

དོན་དག་	མ་འོངས་པ་	ད་ལྟ་བ་	འདས་པ་	སྐུལ་ཚིག་
Meanings	*Future*	*Present*	*Past*	*Imperative*
to go	འགྲོ་	འགྲོ་	ཕྱིན་	རྒྱུག་ཅིག་
to order	མངག་	མངག་	མངགས་	* * *
to write	འབྲི་	འབྲི་	བྲིས་	བྲིས་ཤིག་
to make	བཟོ་	བཟོ་	བཟོས་	བཟོས་ཤིག་
to jump	མཆོང་	མཆོང་	མཆོངས་	མཆོངས་ཤིག་
to take	འཁྱེར་	འཁྱེར་	ཁྱེར་	ཁྱེར་ཅིག་
to praise	བསྔག་	བསྔག་	བསྔགས་	སྔོགས་ཤིག་
to cut into pieces	གཙབ་	གཙབ་	བཙབས་	བཙོབས་ཤིག་
to close eye etc.	བཙུམ་	བཙུམ་	བཙུམས་	བཙུམས་ཤིག
to cook	བཙོ་	བཙོ་	བཙོས་	འཚོས་ཤིག་
to melt	བཞུ་	བཞུ་	བཞུས་	བཞུ་ཞིག་
to find	རྙེད་	རྙེད་	བརྙེད་	* * *
to copy	བཤུ་	བཤུ་	བཤུས་	བཤུས་ཤིག་
to do	བྱེད་	བྱེད་	བྱས་	བྱེད་ཅིག་
to burn	འཚིག་	འཚིག་	འཚིགས་	* * *
to cut	གཞར་	གཞར་	བཞར་	བཞོར་ཅིག་
(hair)	བཞར་	བཞར་	བཞར་	བཞོར་ཅིག་

དོན་དག་ *Meanings*	མ་འོངས་པ་ *Future*	ད་ལྟ་བ་ *Present*	འདས་པ་ *Past*	སྐུལ་ཚིག་ *Imperative*
to cut (bread etc.)	གཏུབ་	གཏུབ་	བཏུབས་	བཏུབས་ཤིག་
to read	ཀློག་	ཀློག་	བཀླགས་	ཀློགས་ཤིག་
to get up	ལང་	ལང་	ལངས་	ལོངས་ཤིག་
to cover	གཏུམ་	གཏུམ་	བཏུམས་	བཏུམས་ཤིག་
to climb	འཛེག་	འཛེག་	འཛེགས་	འཛེགས་ཤིག་
to open (mouth etc.)	གདང་	གདང་	གདངས་	གདོངས་ཤིག་
to cover or to put on clothes	གཡོག་	གཡོག་	གཡོགས་	གཡོགས་ཤིག་
to throw (any liquid)	གཞོ་	གཞོ་	བཞོས་	བཞོས་ཤིག་
to dance	འཁྲབ་	འཁྲབ་	འཁྲབས་	ཁྲོབས་ཤིག་
to catch	འཛུ་	འཛུ་	འཛུས་	འཛུས་ཤིག་
to ask	འདྲི་	འདྲི་	དྲིས་	དྲིས་ཤིག་
to snatch	འཕྲོག་	འཕྲོག་	ཕྲོགས་	ཕྲོགས་ཤིག་
to call	འབོད་	འབོད་	བོས་	བོས་ཤིག་
to rent	གླ་	གླ་	གླས་	གློས་ཤིག་
to cry	ངུ་	ངུ་	ངུས་	ངུས་ཤིག་
to bury/ hide	སྦ་	སྦ་	སྦས་	སྦོས་ཤིག་

དོན་དག་ Meanings	མ་འོངས་པ་ Future	ད་ལྟ་བ་ Present	འདས་པ་ Past	སྐུལ་ཚིག་ Imperative
to hide	ཡིབ་	ཡིབ་	ཡིབས་	ཡིབས་ཤིག་
to buy	ཉོ་	ཉོ་	ཉོས་	ཉོས་ཤིག་
to give	སྦྱོད་	སྦྱོད་	སྦྱད་	སྦྱོད་ཅིག་
to distribute	འགྲིམས་	འགྲིམས་	བཀྲམས་	ཁྲིམས་ཤིག་

The future and present remain the same in the above verbs.

དོན་དག་ *Meanings*	མ་འོངས་པ་ *Future*	ད་ལྟ་བ་ *Present*	འདས་པ་ *Past*	སྐུལ་ཚིག་ *Imperative*
to study / learn / practice	སྦྱང་	སྦྱོང་	སྦྱངས་	སྦྱོངས་་
to send	གཏང་	གཏོང་	བཏང་	གཏོང་ཞིག་
to exchange	བརྗེ་	རྗེ་	བརྗེས་	བརྗེས་ཤིག་
to take	ལེན་	ལླང་	ལླངས་	ལོངས་ཤིག་
to watch	བལྟ་	ལྟ་	བལྟས་	ལྟོས་ཤིག་
to stay / live / sit	བསྡད་	སྡོད་	བསྡད་	སྡོད་ཅིག་
to forget	བརྗེད་	རྗེད་	བརྗེད་	* * *
to sell	བཙོང་	འཚོང་	བཙོངས་	ཚོངས་ཤིག་
to get lost	བརླག་	རླག་	བརླགས་	* * *
to tell	བཤད་	ཤོད་	བཤད་	ཤོད་ཅིག་
to stitch	བཙེམ་	འཚེམ་	བཙེམས་	འཚེམས་ཤིག་
to put on	བསྐོན་	སྐོན་	བསྐོན་	སྐོན་ཅིག་
to divide	བགོ་	བགོད་	བགོས་	བགོས་ཤིག་
to meditate	བསྒོམ་	སྒོམ་	བསྒོམས་	སྒོམས་ཤིག་

དོན་དག་	མ་འོངས་པ་	ད་ལྟ་བ་	འདས་པ་	སྐུལ་ཚིག་
Meanings	*Future*	*Present*	*Past*	*Imperative*
to translate	བསྒྱུར་	སྒྱུར་	བསྒྱུར་	སྒྱུར་ཅིག་
to pick up	བསྒྲུག་	སྒྲུག་	བསྒྲུགས་	སྒྲུགས་ཤིག་
to drink	བཏུང་	འཐུང་	བཏུངས་	ཐུངས་ཤིག་
to smell	བསྣམ་	སྣམ་	བསྣམས་	སྣོམས་ཤིག་
to find out	བཙལ་	འཚོལ་	བཙལ་	འཚོལ་ཤིག་
to kill	གསད་	གསོད་	བསད་	གསོད་ཅིག་
to erase	བསུབ་	སུབ་	བསུབས་	བསུབས་ཤིག་
to protect	བསྲུང་	སྲུང་	བསྲུངས་	སྲུངས་ཤིག་
to teach	བསླབ་	སློབ་	བསླབས་	སློབས་ཤིག་
to beg	བསླང་	སློང་	བསླངས་	སློངས་ཤིག་
to wash	བཀྲུ་	འཁྲུད་	བཀྲུས་	ཁྲུས་ཤིག་
to beat / knock	བརྡུང་	རྡུང་	བརྡུངས་	རྡུངས་ཤིག་
to wait	བསྒུག་	སྒུག་	བསྒུགས་	སྒུགས་ཤིག་

དོན་དག་	མ་འོངས་པ་	ད་ལྟ་བ་	འདས་པ་	སྐུལ་ཚིག་
Meanings	*Future*	*Present*	*Past*	*Imperative*
to fry	རྔོ་	རྔོད་	བརྔོས་	བརྔོས་ཤིག
to cut	གཅད་	གཅོད་	བཅད་	ཆོད་ཅིག་
to break	གཅག་	གཅོག་	བཅག་	ཆོག་ཅིག་
to steal	བརྐུ་	རྐུ་	བརྐུས་	རྐུས་ཤིག་
to save	བསྐྱབ་	སྐྱོབ་	བསྐྱབས་	སྐྱོབས་ཤིག་
to borrow	བསྐྱི་	སྐྱི་	བསྐྱིས་	སྐྱིས་ཤིག་
to send	བསྐུར་	སྐུར་	བསྐུར་	སྐུར་ཅིག་
to boil	བསྐོལ་	སྐོལ་	བསྐོལ་	སྐོལ་ཅིག་

The verbs in the future, present & past are not the same but in some cases the future and past remain the same in the above given verbs.

COMMON IDIOMS :

ལྷག་གེ་ལྷུག་གེ་	lose / hospitable
ཐྲ་མེ་ཐྲོམ་མེ་	befuddled / dazed
ཐྲར་རེ་ཐྲོར་རེ་	few / some / scattered
ཁྲིགས་ཁྲིགས་	untrustworthy
ཉ་རེ་ཉོ་རེ་	not solid / runny
ལྷ་རེ་ལྷུ་རེ་	not solid / runny
ལྷ་མེ་ལྷེམ་མེ་	flexible
ཡམ་མེ་ཡོམ་མེ་	weak / faint
ལྷབ་བེ་ལྷོབ་བེ་	lose (of things only)
ཙ་གེ་ཙིག་གེ་	small things
འཚབ་བེ་འཚུབ་བེ་	hyperactive / in a hurry
ཚ་གེ་ཚིག་གེ་	hyperactive / in a hurry
འབལ་ལེ་འབོལ་ལེ་	soft / plenty
འབར་རེ་འབུར་རེ་	bumpy /inconsistent
འ་རེ་འུར་རེ་	noisy / a hue & cry
སྐད་ཅོར་ཆ་པོ་	noisy
ཀར་རེ་ཀོར་རེ་	excuse /by twists & turns
ཉ་གེ་ཉིག་གེ་	sloppy / untidy / dirty

ཉ་ག་ཉོག་ག་	sloppy / disorderly
ཀྱག་ག་ཀྱོག་ག་	zigzag
སྦ་བེ་སྦེབ་བེ་	scant
སྦ་བེ་སྦོབ་བེ་	soft and fine
ཉ་བེ་ཉོབ་བེ་	lazy / inactive
ཧ་རེ་ཧོ་རེ་	carelessly
ཧ་བེ་ཧོབ་བེ་	in a hurry / carelessly
ཧྲག་ག་ཧྲུག་ག་	small pieces
ཡང་ནས་ཡང་དུ་	again and again
ཁྱུར་རེ་ཁྱུར་རེ་	unstable / weak
ཕར་ཡོ་ཚུར་ཡོ་	unstable
ཁྲ་ག་ཁྲུག་ག་	unrest
ཚ་ག་ཚི་ག་	restless / excited
ཛ་རེ་ཛོ་རེ་	untidy / sloppy
ཟང་ངེ་ཟིང་ངེ་	unrest / sloppy / hustle & bustle
གང་བྱུང་མང་བྱུང་	irregular / disorderly
དང་དུ་ལེན་པ་	to promise / voluntarily
ནན་ཏན་	emphatic
བྲེལ་བ་ཚ་པོ་	busy
སྤུས་དག་པོ་	good quality

ཁྱོན་ནས་མེད་	don't have at all
མཐོང་རྒྱ་ཆེན་པོ་	broad mind
གཏིང་རིང་པོ་	deep
རྒྱ་ཆེན་པོ་	wide
གུ་ཡངས་པོ་	broad
གལ་ཆེན་པོ་	important
ལྟ་ཅི་སྨོས་	needless to say
དཔེ་མི་སྲིད་པའི་ཡག་པོ་	very good / extremely good
དཔེ་མི་སྲིད་པའི་སྡུག་ཅག་	very bad / extremely bad
ཧ་ཅང་མཛེས་པོ་	very beautiful / extremely beautiful
ཧ་ཅང་མདོག་ཉེས་པོ་	very ugly
སྙིང་རྗེ་པོ་	pretty / good / interesting
ཁ་ཁྱུ་སིམ་པོ་	quite
ཡར་རྒྱས་གོང་འཕེལ་	progress

LETTER WRITING

When a letter is written in Tibetan, the place, the sender's name, the year and the date should be placed at conclusion of the letter.

Here are some examples showing the traditional ways of beginning and ending letters :

BEGINNING :

༄༅། བརྗེ་བའི་གྲོགས་མཆོག་ name ལགས་ཀྱི་སྐུ་དྲུང་དུ།

༄༅། བརྗེ་བའི་གྲོགས་མཆོག་དམ་པ་ * * ལགས་གང་དྲུང་དུ།

༄༅། སྙིང་ནས་བརྗེ་བའི་ * * * * * ལགས་ཀྱི་དྲུང་དུ།

༄༅། ཤིན་ཏུ་བརྗེ་བའི་ * * * * * * ལགས་གང་དེ་ར།

༄༅། མཆུངས་མེད་སྐུ་ཞབས་ * * * * མཆོག་ལ།

END :

དབྱིན་ཡུལ་ནས་ཕྲན་ name ནས་ ༡༩༩༠ ཕྱི་ཟླ་ཚེས་ལ།
ཕུལ།།

ད་རམ་ས་ལ་ནས་ཕྲན་ * * * ནས་ ༩༠ ཕྱི་ཟླ་ཚེས་ལ།
ཕུལ།།

EXAMPLES OF LETTERS :

1. [A letter to a friend asking him/her to reserve a room.]

༄༅། བརྩེ་བའི་གྲོགས་མཆོག་ name ལགས་ཀྱི་དྲུང་དུ།

ཆེད་ཞུ། སྐུ་ཉིད་

ཞལ་མཇལ་མ་བྱུང་བར་སྐུ་ཁམས་སྔར་བཞིན་གསལ་དྭངས་ཡོད་ཤག་རེད། ད་ལྟའི་ཆར་ང་རང་བོད་ཀྱི་རྒྱལ་རབས་སྐོར་དེབ་ཞིག་ཕྱོགས་སྒྲིག་བྱེད་བཞིན་ཡོད། རྩ་བའི་ང་རང་ནས་ལོ་དྲུག་གི་རིང་བོད་ཀྱི་རྒྱལ་རབས་ཐོག་ཉམས་ཞིབ་བྱས་པ་ཡིན། དེར་བརྟེན་སླར་ཡང་ང་རང་བོད་ཀྱི་དཔེ་མཛོད་ཁང་དུ་ཟླ་གསུམ་རིང་རྒྱལ་རབས་ཉམས་ཞིབ་དང་། རྒྱལ་རབས་མཁས་པའི་མི་སྣ་འགའ་ཤས་མཇལ་འཕྲད་ཞུ་དགོས་པ་སོགས་ཀྱི་ཆེད་དབྱིན་ཡུལ་ནས་ ༩༠ ཕྱི་ཟླ་བཅུ་པའི་ཚེས་བཅུ་ཉིན་རྒྱ་གར་དུ་ཐོན་རྒྱུ་ཡིན་པས་ང་རང་སྡོད་ཡུལ་ཁང་གླ་ཆེ་ཆུང་ལ་མ་ལྟོས་པར་ཁང་མིག་ཞིག་ཐོབ་ཐབས་ཡོང་བ་ཞུ་རྒྱུ་དང་། གལ་ཏེ་སྡོད་ཡུལ་ཁང་གླ་མ་ཐོབ་ཚེ་གཤམ་གསལ་ཁ་བྱང་ཐོག་གནས་ལན་ཞིག་གནང་རོགས་ཞུ་རྒྱུ་བཅས། དབྱིན་ཡུལ་ནས་གྲོགས་མིང་ ____________________ གིས་

༡༩༩༠ ཕྱི་ཟླ་ཚེས་ལ།

ཕུལ།།

Vocabulary :

སྐུ་ཉིད་	you [h]
ད་ལྟའི་ཆར་	at present
ཕྱོགས་སྒྲིག་བྱེད་བཞིན་པ་	compiling
ཉམས་ཞིབ་	research
དེར་བརྟེན་	therefore
སླར་ཡང་	again
ཟླ་གསུམ་རིང་	for three months
རྒྱལ་རབས་	history
མཁས་པ་	expert
མི་སྣ་	people
ཐོན་རྒྱུ་	to leave
ཁང་གླ་ཆེ་ཆུང་ལ་མ་ལྟོས་པར་	whatever the rent may be
གལ་ཏེ་	incase
མ་ཐོབ་ཆེ་	if it is not possible
སྡོད་ཡུལ་	accomodation / place to stay / room
གཤམ་གསལ་ཁ་བྱང་	below mentioned address
གནས་ལན་	reply
དབྱིན་ཡུལ་	Britain

2. [Reply to the above letter]

༄༅། སྙིང་ནས་བརྩེ་བའི་གྲོགས་མཆོག་ name ལགས་གང་

དྲུང་དུ།

ཆེད་ཞུ། སྐུ་

ཉིད་ནས་བཏང་གནང་བའི་ཕྱག་བྲིས་ཉེ་ཆར་ལག་འབྱོར་བྱུང་བ་

དགའ་པོ་བྱུང་། གནས་ཚུལ་ནང་གསལ་ལྟར། སྐུ་ཉིད་ཀྱི་ཆེད་

ཁང་པ་ཡག་པོ་ཞིག་སླས་ཡོད། ཁང་སླ་ཟླ་རེ་རྒྱ་གར་སྒོར་མོ་དྲུག་

བརྒྱ་ཐམ་པ་འབུལ་རྒྱུ་བྱས་པ་བཅས་དགོངས་འཇགས་ཞུ།

ང་རམ་ས་ལ་ནས་གྲོགས་མིང་ -------------------------- གྱིས་

༡༠ ཕྱི་ཟླ་ཚེས་ལ་

ཕུལ།།

Vocabulary :

ཕྱག་བྲིས་	letter [h]
ཉེ་ཆར་	recently
ལག་འབྱོར་བྱུང་	received
དགའ་པོ་བྱུང་	[I was] happy
གནས་ཚུལ་ནང་གསལ་ལྟར་	as mentioned in the letter
སྐུ་ཉིད་ཀྱི་ཆེད་	for you [h]
ཁང་པ་གླས་	rented
རྒྱ་གར་སྒོར་མོ་	Indian rupees
དྲུག་བརྒྱ་	six hundred
ཐམ་པ་	complete; full- almost exclusively used as a pleonastic addition, to the tens up to a hundred (Das)
འབུལ་རྒྱུ་	to give / to pay [h]
དགོངས་འཇགས་ཞུ་	please keep [it] in mind [h]

3. [A letter from a sister to her elder brother.]

༄༅། བརྩེ་བའི་ཇོ་ལགས་ name ལགས་ཀྱི་སྐུ་དྲུང་དུ།

སྙབས་ཞུ།

ཇོ་ལགས་ཞལ་མཇལ་མ་བྱུང་བར་ཟླ་ཤས་སོང་བ་སྐུ་གཟུགས་བདེ་ཐང་ཡོད་ཤག་རེད། འདིར་ཡང་ང་རང་གཟུགས་པོ་བདེ་ཐང་དང་ ཇ་རམ་ས་ལའི་བོད་ཀྱི་དཔེ་མཛོད་ཁང་དུ་ནང་ཆོས་དང་། བོད་ཀྱི་སྐད་ཡིག་སུ་མཐུད་ནས་སློབ་སྦྱོང་བྱེད་ཀྱི་ཡོད། ད་ལྟའི་ཆར་བོད་ཀྱི་སྐད་ཡིག་ཐོག་ཡར་རྒྱས་གང་འཚམས་ཕྱིན་ཡོད། ད་དུང་ཟླ་ཤས་སློབ་སྦྱོང་བྱས་རྗེས་བོད་ཀྱི་སྐད་ཡིག་ཡག་ཐག་ཆོད་ཤེས་ཐུབ་པའི་རེ་བ་ཡོད་ སླད་ཞལ་མཇལ་མ་བྱུང་བར་སྐུ་གཟུགས་ལ་ཐུགས་ཅག་གང་ཟབ་གནང་རོགས་ཞུ་རྒྱུ་བཅས། ཇ་རམ་ས་ལ་ནས་གཅུང་མོ་________________ནས་ ༡༠ ཕྱི་ཟླ་ཚེས་ལ་

ཕུལ།།

Vocabulary :

ཟླ་ཤས་སོང་བ་	a few months passed
བདེ་ཐང་	well / fine
འདིར་ཡང་	here / also here
ནང་ཆོས་	dharma / Buddhism
བོད་ཀྱི་སྐད་ཡིག་	Tibetan language
མུ་མཐུད་ནས་	continuously
སློབ་སྦྱོང་བྱེད་ཀྱི་ཡོད་	studying
ད་ལྟའི་ཆར་	at present / right now
ཡར་རྒྱས་	progress
གང་འཚམས་	quite a bit
ད་དུང་	still
ཡག་ཐག་ཆོད་	good enough
ཤེས་ཐུབ་པ་	able to know
རེ་བ་	hope
སླད་	later / in future / untill
ཐུགས་ཅག་* གང་ཟབ་	good care [h]
གཅུང་མོ་	younger sister

---

* ཅག་ནི། ཁྱེད་ཅག་ ང་ཅག་སོགས་དང་ ཅ་གའི་བསྡུས་ཚིག

4. [Reply to the above letter.]

༄༅། ཤིན་ཏུ་བརྩེ་བའི་གཅུང་མོ་ name གང་དེ་ར།
ཁྱེད་ཀྱི་གནས་ཚུལ་ལག་འབྱོར་བྱུང་བ་ཧ་ཅང་དགའ་པོ་བྱུང་།
འདིར་ཡང་ང་རང་དང་། ཡབ་ཡུམ་གཉིས་བཅས་བདེ་པོ་ཡིན།
ཁྱེད་རང་བོད་ཀྱི་ནང་ཆོས་དང་། སྐད་ཡིག་ལ་མུ་མཐུད་ནས་སློབ་
སྦྱོང་གནང་ཐུབ་པ་དགའ་པོ་ཞི་དྲག་བྱུང་། རྗེས་སུ་དུས་ཚོད་ཐོབ་
མཚམས་ང་རང་ཡང་བོད་ཀྱི་ནང་ཆོས་དང་། སྐད་ཡིག་སློབ་སྦྱོང་
བྱེད་ཐུབ་པའི་རེ་བ་ཡོད། མ་མཇལ་བར་ཁྱེད་རང་སྐུ་གཟུགས་ལ་
ཐུགས་ཅག་དང་། འདིར་བློ་བདེའི་ཕྱག་བྲིས་ཡང་ཡང་ཡོད་པ་
བཅས། ཨ་རི་ནས་གཅེན་པོས་ ༡༠ ཕྱི་ཟླ་ཚེས་ལ།

ཕུལ།།

Vocabulary :

ཤིན་ཏུ་བརྩེ་བ་	dearest
ཧ་ཅང་	extremely
འདིར་	here
ཡབ་ཡུམ་	parents [h]
བདེ་པོ་	well / fine
ཐུབ་པ་	able to

དགའ་པོ་ཞི་དྲག་	very happy
རྗེས་སུ་	later
བློ་བདེའི་ཕྱག་བྲིས་	a letter of reassurance
ཡང་ཡང་	again and again
གཅེན་པོ་	elder brother
དུས་ཚོད་ཐོབ་མཚམས་	when [I] get time

---

5. [A letter to the Secretary enquiring about the Tibetan language courses at the Centre for Tibetan Studies, Dharamsala.]

༄༅། མཆུངས་མེད་སྐུ་ཞབས་ name མཆོག་ལ།

ཆེད་ཞུ། ང་རང་བོད་ཀྱི་
སྐད་ཡིག་སློབ་སྦྱོང་བྱེད་འདོད་ཧ་ཅང་ཆེ་བར་བརྟེན། དེ་ག་བོད་ཀྱི་
དཔེ་མཛོད་ཁང་དུ་ལོ་གཅིག་གི་རིང་སྐད་ཡིག་སློབ་སྦྱོང་གི་ཆེད་བཅར་
རྒྱུས་ཡིན་ན། དེ་གར་སྐད་ཡིག་འཛིན་གྲྭ་དབུ་འཛུགས་ག་དུས་
གནང་གི་ཡོད་མེད་དང་། ཉིན་རེ་འཛིན་གྲྭ་ཆུ་ཚོད་ག་ཚད་ཚུགས་
གནང་གི་ཡོད་མེད། སློབ་དེབ་བེད་སྤྱོད་ག་རེ་གནང་གི་ཡོད་མེད་

བཅས་འཁོད་པའི་གནས་ཚུལ་ཁ་གསལ་ཞིག་གཤམ་གསལ་ཁ་

སྒྲིང་ཐོག་ངེས་པར་དུ་གནང་སྐྱོངས་ཡོད་པ་དགོངས་འཇགས་ཞུ།

ཉི་ཧོང་ནས་____________གིས་ ༡༠ ཕྱི་ཟླ་ཚེས་ལ།

ཕུལ།།

Vocabulary :

སློབ་སྦྱོང་བྱེད་འདོད་	wanted to study
བརྟེན་	therefore
བོད་ཀྱི་དཔེ་མཛོད་ཁང་	Tibetan Library
ལོ་གཅིག་གི་རིང་	for one year
བཅར་	come [h]
འཛིན་གྲྭ་	class
དབུ་འཛུགས་	start / begin [h]
ཉིན་རེ་	everyday / each day
ཆུ་ཚོད་	hour
ག་ཚད་	how many / how much
སློབ་དེབ་	textbook
བེད་སྤྱོད་	use
འཁོད་པ་	mentioned
ངེས་པར་དུ་	must

6. [Reply to the above letter.]

༄༅། མཚུངས་མེད་སྐུ་ཞབས་ name མཆོག་ལ།

ཆེད་ཞུ། སྐུ་ཉིད་ནས་

༡༠ ཕྱི་ཟླ་ཚེས་ཉིན་བཏང་གནང་བའི་ཕྱག་བྲིས་ལག་འབྱོར་བྱུང་ཞིང་། ཕྱག་བྲིས་ནང་གསལ་ལྟར། འདི་ག་བོད་ཀྱི་དཔེ་མཛོད་ཁང་གི་སྐད་ཡིག་འཛིན་གྲྭ་འཆར་ཅན་ཕྱི་ཟླ་གསུམ་པའི་ནང་དབུ་འཛུགས་ཞུ་གི་ཡོད་པ་དང་། དེ་ཡང་ཉིན་རེ་སློབ་ཡུན་ཆུ་ཚོད་གཅིག་དང་། སློབ་དེབ་ཁག་སྐུ་ཉིད་རྒྱ་གར་དུ་ཕེབས་མཚམས་ད་རམ་ས་ལར་སྤུས་གཟིགས་གནང་ན་འགྲིགས་འདུས་བཅས་དགོངས་འཇགས་ཞུ། བོད་ཀྱི་དཔེ་མཛོད་ཁང་ནས་ ༡༠ ཕྱི་ཟླ་ཚེས་ལ།

ཕུལ།།

Vocabulary :

སྐད་ཡིག་འཛིན་གྲྭ་	language class
འཆར་ཅན་	regularly
དབུ་འཛུགས་	start / begin [h]

དེ་ཡང་	that too
ཉིན་རེ་	everyday
སློབ་ཡུན་	study time / period
ཆུ་ཚོད་	hour / watch
སྐུས་གཟིགས་	to buy [h]

Important Note

༄། སྤྱིར་བཏང་ཕལ་སྐད་ཐོག་ཕན་ཚུན་བཀའ་མོལ་གནང་སྐབས་བརྗོད་བདེའི་དབང་གིས་འབྲེལ་སྒྲའི་སྦྱོར་ཚུལ་གཤམ་གསལ་རིའུ་མིག་ལྟར་ཡང་སེ་བེད་སྤྱོད་གནང་མིན་ཡང་། རྩ་བའི་སུམ་ཅུ་པའི་གཞུང་ལྟར་གཤམ་བཀོད་རིའུ་མིག་ལྟར་བེད་སྤྱོད་གནང་རྒྱུ་ཤིན་ཏུ་གལ་ཆེའོ།།

In general, in ordinary colloquial Tibetan the grammatical rules of sentence construction for genitives and possessives are not followed strictly, especially when such construction would impede the ease of movement of the tongue. Nevertheless, it is important to know these grammatical rules, which are summarized on the chart below.

འབྲེལ་སྒྲ་སྦྱོར་ཚུལ་གྱི་རེའུ་མིག

A chart of genitives with examples:

རྗེས་འཇུག་ Suffixes	འབྲེལ་སྒྲ་ Particles	སྦྱོར་ཚུལ་ Examples
ག་ ང་	གི་	གཡག་གི་རྭ་ཅོ། ཕོང་གི་ཕྱུག་རིབ།
ད་ བ་ ས་	ཀྱི་	ཁྱེད་ཀྱི་གྲོགས་པོ། དེབ་ཀྱི་མིང་། གཡས་ཀྱི་གངས་རི།
ན་ མ་ ར་ ལ་	གྱི་	གཡོན་གྱི་རི། ལམ་གྱི་དཀྱིལ། དངུར་གྱི་མེ་ཏོག བལ་གྱི་ཞྭ་མོ།
འ་ དང་ མཐའ་མེད་	འི་ དང་ ཡི་	ནམ་མཁའི་ཁ་མདོག ནམ་མཁའ་ཡི་ཁ་མདོག ངའི་ཁང་པ། ང་ཡི་ཁང་པ།

ལ་དོན་གྱི་རེའུ་མིག

A chart of accusative, dative and locative cases:

རྗེས་འཇུག་ Suffixes	ཕྲད Particles	སྦྱོར་ཚུལ་ Examples
ས་	སུ་	རྗེས་སུ། ཕྱོགས་སུ།
ག་ བ་ ད་དྲག	ཏུ་	རྟག་ཏུ། དེབ་ཏུ། ཤིནད་ཏུ།
ང་ ད་ ན་ མ་ ར་ ལ་	དུ་	བྱང་དུ། བོད་དུ། གཞན་དུ། མཉམ་དུ། རྒྱ་གར་དུ། བལ་ཡུལ་དུ།
འ་ དང་ མཐའ་མེད་	ར་ དང་ རུ་	མཐར་འགྱོལ། མཐའ་རུ་འགྱོལ། ལྷ་སར། ལྷ་ས་རུ།

རྒྱན་སྡུད་ཀྱི་ཕྲད་རྣམས་སྦྱོར་ཚུལ་རེའུ་མིག

Conjunction:

རྗེས་འཇུག་ Suffixes	ཕྲད་ Particles	སྦྱོར་ཚུལ་ Examples
ག་ ད་ བ་ ས་ ད་དྲག	ཀྱང་	བཀག་ཀྱང་། ཡོད་ཀྱང་། གཟབ་ཀྱང་། ཞེབས་ཀྱང་། བསྟན་ཀྱང་།
ང་ ན་ མ་ ལ་ ར་	ཡང་	ཆང་ཡང་། གཞན་ཡང་། འཆམ་ཡང་། བལ་ཡང་། འཕར་ཡང་།
འ་ དང་ མཐའ་མེད་	འང་ དང་ ཡང་	དགའང་། དགའ་ཡང་། དེའང་། དེ་ཡང་།